What Every Mom Needs

Balancing Your Life

by Elisa Morgan & Carol Kuykendall
with Bible Study Activities by Betty Hassler

LifeWay Press
Nashville, Tennessee

LifeWay
© Copyright 1999 MOPS International, Inc.
All Rights Reserved
Reprint 2001

ISBN 0-7673-9373-2
Dewey Decimal Classification: 305.4
Subject Heading: MOTHERS—RELIGIOUS LIFE/WOMEN—RELIGIOUS LIFE

This book is the text for Course CG-0479 in the subject area Personal Life
in the Christian Growth Study Plan

Unless otherwise indicated, Scripture references are from the Holy Bible,
New International Version, © copyright 1973, 1978, 1984 by International Bible Society.

To order additional copies of this resource: WRITE LifeWay Church Resources Customer Service, 127 Ninth Avenue, North,
Nashville, TN 37234-0113; FAX order to (615) 251-5933; PHONE 1-800-458-2772; EMAIL to *CustomerService@lifeway.com*
ONLINE at *www.lifeway.com*; or visit the LifeWay Christian Store serving you.

LifeWay Christian Resources vision statement:
As God works through us, we will help people and churches know Jesus Christ and seek His kingdom
by providing biblical solutions that spiritually transform individuals and cultures.

Betty Hassler, Design Editor
Paula Savage, Art Director
Pam Shepherd, Assistant Editor
Rhonda Porter Delph, Manuscript Assistant

Printed in the United States of America

☥

LifeWay Press
127 Ninth Avenue, North
Nashville, Tennessee 37234-0151

Contents

Introduction

"I should have known going to the grocery store wouldn't work today," Linda scolded herself as she placed two-month-old Jason into the infant seat of the cart. Already, he was fussing, and she felt embarrassed and guilty as he whimpered all the way through the produce section.

She checked her watch. Almost 2:30. No wonder he was fussy. He should be home in his crib asleep. Yet, in between feedings and quick naps, it had taken her all day to get the baby and herself ready to go to the store.

What was wrong with her? Since becoming a mother, she'd totally lost control of her time. She used to be able to make a list and accomplish tasks efficiently. When she was pregnant, she'd pictured herself getting everything done and still having time for herself. Now she barely got out of the house to run a single errand—like going to the grocery store—which, if she could pull it off, would probably turn out to be her one accomplishment of the day. Big whoop!

Maybe, if she cut her list in half and bought only milk, diapers, and something for dinner, she could finish quickly. She headed for the frozen food section. What else was on her list? Oh, no, the list! She rummaged frantically through her purse. She must have left it on the kitchen counter. She sighed and pushed the cart faster.

By the time she got to the dairy products, Jason had worked his fussing into pitiful wails. Everyone within 30 feet was watching as she tried to comfort him—with no success. She finally made it through the checkout line, wheeled her groceries and Jason to the car, strapped him in, and drove home. He finally calmed down and, a few blocks from home, she faced another problem. Exhausted from the outing, he was about to fall asleep.

Oh, no! She needed to get him home, feed him, and put him down for a real nap so she would have time to unload and put away the groceries and think about dinner before he woke up again. She shook a rattle while loudly singing his name until they pulled up in front of the house.

Quickly, Linda unbuckled herself and then Jason, slung the diaper bag and purse over her shoulder, and heaved the infant seat up in front of her. She resisted the urge to grab a sack of groceries as well and trudged up the steps.

Once inside, she dumped her load on the table, whisked the baby to the bedroom and changed his diaper. Rocking him while he ate, she tried to enjoy the moment. This was the image she had envisioned when she dreamed about becoming a mother—soft moments like this, holding a serene child, the whole focus of her life.

But now thoughts of melting groceries, dinner, and doing more laundry blocked any feelings of serenity. Tears suddenly formed under her heavy eyelids. She felt so tired—more tired and discouraged and alone than ever before in her whole life. She thought she could handle being a mom. She thought she'd know how to do it. But this wasn't what she'd expected. This was, well, it was so *hard!*

What's the matter with me? Linda wondered.

Expectations Versus Reality

Most likely, you've felt like Linda. Maybe, for you, it was last month or last week. Maybe it was an hour ago. Whenever it occurs, this disappointment, confusion, and sense of inadequacy is surprising. Mothering isn't supposed to be this way!

In the days prior to actually becoming mothers, we imagine motherhood swathed in perfect pastels. Then reality hits.

My dreams and expectations were along the lines of a diaper commercial—lots of smiles and coos and a perfectly happy and contented baby. Sure, there would be difficult times, but they would not get me down for long. And my love for my baby would overcome any lack of sleep or missed lunches with my girlfriends. Not so, I've learned.

A second mom dreamed, *I thought my child and I would be perfect together. I pictured myself looking great when my husband came home. We'd sit down to a well-balanced meal, followed by family strolls in the park and quiet romantic evenings while baby slept. What a joke!*

Only a few months into mothering, we face the disappointing gap between our expectations and the rock-hard reality of being on duty 24 hours a day, engaged in some of the most unseemly aspects of life.

Yes, of course there are wonderful, tender moments. Even whole hours of bliss! Caressing petal-soft skin. Fingering perfect miniature hands, dimpled at the knuckles. Smooching under chins, behind ears, and smack-dab in the center of plump cheeks. Yes, there are wondrous times in mothering!

And there are also shocking, unexpected days and weeks. These are the times we quickly come to the end of who we are and what we know, and we wonder how we're going to make it through the next 20 years ... or 20 minutes.

Moms Have Needs Too!

As mothers of children from infancy to school age, we find a widening gap between our expectations and the reality of our day-to-day lives. In this gap lie some of our most insistent, basic needs—to sleep, to grow, to talk with someone who cares. To regain perspective and find hope. Yet because of the demanding, hectic nature of our days, we don't often examine those needs, much less take time to meet them.

Ignoring those needs not only jeopardizes the health and well-being of the mom but of the whole family. This book is about what moms need. We make two main points:

1. *Moms have needs.* As we begin to discuss them in specific, it's important that we understand them in general.

   —Needs are normal. Psychologists and social scientists and religious experts agree that all normal people have needs and healthy people recognize these needs. A mom who believes that she has no important needs is sure to end up feeling frustrated and empty.

   —Needs are personal. Some of your needs will be greater than others. Your needs may differ from those of your best friend. In some moments, one need may seem much greater than another and then, in the very next hour, they may trade places in importance.

   —Needs must be recognized. Needs are nagging and insistent. They don't like to be ignored. If they don't receive the attention they demand in a healthy manner, they're apt to rear their heads in undesirable behavior, such as anxiety, depression, or temper.

2. *Moms must learn to recognize and meet their own needs in order to better meet the needs of their children.* Sitting through preflight instructions on an airplane, you are told that if the oxygen masks drop down during flight and you are flying with a small child, you should first affix the oxygen mask to your own face and then assist the child. The implication is obvious: you can't help a child to breathe if you've fainted from your own lack of oxygen!

   Similarly, moms cannot effectively meet the needs of their children while ignoring their own. Moms must recognize the value of understanding and meeting their own needs for the sake of their children and families.

Nine Needs

Each week's study represents one of the 9 needs unique to the stage of life in which we mother children from infancy to school age. These needs were identified by MOPS International, an organization that has been reaching out to mothers of preschoolers and meeting their needs since 1973, now in every state of the United States and in 11 other countries. The compilation of these needs came through years of research, interviews, and experience with mothers of preschoolers, in addition to 1000 questionnaires sent to moms in MOPS groups around the country. Their responses are shared throughout this book.

You'll notice that when a mom speaks, we have not introduced her or identified her. Instead, her voice is set apart in italics or printed in the margin. It is our hope that you will make friends with the women revealed in these pages. Perhaps you will recognize someone you know, possibly even yourself.

Whether you work full-time inside the home or are employed outside as well, whether married or single, whatever your faith heritage, no matter your past or your present, whether you have three children or one, whether you are 19 or 42—this book is for you because these 9 needs describe you.

How to Use This Resource

This Bible study is written as an interactive workbook. It differs from the original book from MOPS International because of the addition of Bible study questions, highlighted with the symbol ✿, and learning activities, identified with the daisy symbol ✿. Because MOPS groups are based on lifestyle evangelism and are not Bible studies, in the MOPS setting, this workbook would be appropriate for off-week Bible studies that grow out of MOPS groups.

 Use the workbook like you would a personal diary or journal. Write in it. Underline key ideas and phrases. Mark the pages you want to reread. Many responses you will want to share voluntarily with your Bible study group. Others will be personal. Inform family members that your workbook is off limits unless you give permission. (Yes, that includes husbands!) You will want to keep your workbook in a private place.

 As you begin each lesson, remember the most important part: begin in prayer. God will reveal so much more to you when you first ask Him to do so in prayer.

Using This Resource in a Group Setting

You will benefit much more from this Bible study if you participate in a group. The Bible study group leader guide begins on page 120. Complete each week's study and then meet with a group to process your work.

 Some groups will choose to commit each week's featured Scripture to memory. This verse is printed on the title page for each week. A *Mothering Maxim*, also found on the first page of each weekly lesson, helps to condense the main ideas into one memorable statement. Consider memorizing these as well.

Let's Get Started

Each week's material may be studied in one sitting, or it may be read a portion a day over five or six days until the next group meeting. If you are reading a few pages a day, time your reading (read for 10-15 minutes and draw a line where you stop) or read from subhead to subhead (the cherry red titles centered on the page). Remember, don't skip the learning activities. They are designed to help you personalize this study and make specific follow-up plans for what you learn.

 We assure you that you're not alone in your mothering role. We pray you will find encouragement and hope in these pages.

About the Writers

Elisa Morgan and Carol Kuykendall partner together at MOPS International, an outreach providing nurturance and instruction to some two million mothers of preschoolers through MOPS groups, the radio ministry, *MomSense*, and publications such as this book. Individually, Elisa has authored *Mom to Mom*, *Meditations for Mothers*, and *Mom's Devotional Bible*. Carol has written *Learning to Let Go*, *Give Them Wings*, and *A Mother's Footprints of Faith*. This is the third offering of their co-authored projects, the first two being *What Every Mom Needs* and *What Every Child Needs*. A fourth project is *When Husband and Wife Become Mom and Dad*. Elisa lives in Aurora, Colorado with her husband, Evan, and their children, Eva and Ethan. Carol and her husband, Lynn, have three grown children, Derek, Lindsay, and Kendall, and live in Boulder, Colorado.

Betty Hassler contributed the Bible study activities and leader guide for the workbook edition of *What Every Mom Needs*. Betty is a Design Editor/Team Leader at LifeWay Christian Resources, where she edits materials for discipleship, family life, and support group ministries. Betty co-authored *Covenant Marriage: Partnership and Commitment* and *Communication and Intimacy: Covenant Marriage*. She and her husband, Sim, live in Nashville, Tennesse, and have two grown sons, Scott and Mark.

What Every Mom Needs

Meet Your Nine Basic Needs (and Be a Better Mom), is the basis for the workbook edition: *What Every Mom Needs: Balancing Your Life.*

Available at LifeWay Christian Stores
and by
Calling 1-800-233-1123

ZondervanPublishingHouse
Grand Rapids, Michigan

A Division of HarperCollins*Publishers*

Week 1

Significance

Sometimes I Wonder If Mothering Matters

Joanie padded from the refrigerator back to the couch where her recently new-born daughter lay, wrapped in a blanket. Joanie scooped up the baby and cuddled her closely. *So tiny!* But so much bigger than just two months before when the doctor had plopped her on Joanie's stomach in the delivery room. That was a moment she'd never forget.

Joanie touched Marcy's cheek tenderly, then lifted her above her head in a playful mood. "I love you, dear child, more than I ever imagined."

She continued to nuzzle the baby until she heard the familiar theme song of a television newscast. *Five o'clock! Where did the day go? I'm not even dressed,* Joanie thought, glancing down at her wrinkled flannel nightgown. *I've accomplished absolutely nothing today. And I used to be so organized and efficient.*

As a dental hygienist, she had really enjoyed helping people. She'd talk on and on while working on their teeth, then line up the sterilized instruments, ready for the next day. By five o'clock, she knew exactly what she'd accomplished.

But what had she accomplished today? She'd taken care of the baby—bathed, dressed, and fed and fed and fed her. She'd straightened the family room, washed and folded two loads of laundry. Didn't seem like much. But somehow it had consumed her entire day. She hadn't even taken a shower because Marcy woke up just as she turned on the water, and she wasn't yet comfortable taking a shower when the baby was awake.

Only one more month of maternity leave left. How will I ever be able to go back to work when I can't even leave her long enough to take a shower?

This Week's Verse
"Train a child in the way he should go, and when he is old he will not turn from it."
Proverbs 22:6

Mothering Maxim
Mothering matters because today makes a difference tomorrow.

This whole subject of going back to work struck a raw spot in Joanie's heart. Should she go back ... or stay home with Marcy? She didn't know the right answer. John had said they might be able to make it without her salary. But ... could they? Could she?

Just last night at a reception for John's staff, one man had asked Joanie, "So, what do you do?" She'd thought the answer was perfectly obvious as she'd stood there holding her new baby, but the fact that he had asked made her suspect that "I'm a mom" wouldn't do. So she said, "I'm a dental hygienist." The man had brightened and launched into a few dentist jokes.

What would he have said if I'd told him I'm a mom? Joanie mused.

In her heart Joanie wanted nothing more than to be home with Marcy and with any other children she and John might have. But in her head ... she wondered if that would be the right choice. No paycheck. No promotions. No accolades. No to-do list neatly checked off at the end of each day.

Joanie looked down at Marcy, now sleeping in the crook of her arm and again stroked her soft cheek. Could she do this mothering thing? Did mothering really matter enough to invest her life in it?

🍀 Have you had to confront the issue of whether or not to be a working mom?
   (circle)   *Yes*   *No*

🍀 If so, what decision did you make? What factors led to your decision?

_____

_____

🍀 Did the need for personal significance play any role in your decision?
   (circle)   *Yes*   *No*   *Somewhat*

Does Mothering Matter?

We wonder if what we're doing as mothers makes any difference at all.

It's a good question, isn't it? When we're struggling just to get a shower during the daylight hours, we wonder if what we're doing as mothers makes any difference at all. Like darts, negative feelings pierce our confidence and accuse us of insignificance. For example, take the following statements from mothers:

I Feel That What I Do as a Mother Isn't Very Important.
It's tough to see much value in wiping applesauce faces, runny noses, and messy bottoms—not just once—but over and over again. But every mother was once not a

mother. And in her pre-mothering days, she found fulfillment in some aspect of her being—a talent, a career, a sport, a peer group.

Once children arrive on the scene, however, moms must choose between activities. Moms don't receive report cards or yearly job evaluations. Seldom do we receive a pat on the back or an encouraging word about how we're doing or the difference we're making. In fact, sometimes the kids themselves have a way of puncturing our balloons. "Mom, you're mean," they may tell us as we attempt to discipline and guide them. Sometimes we wonder.

❀ Read the following quotes. In the box beside each, indicate if you have experienced these feelings by writing Y (yes), N (no), O (occasionally), or R (rarely).

___*I used to be able to handle a career, run a home, and be a reasonably good wife. I naturally assumed I would be just as effective in mothering. I simply wasn't prepared for feeling inadequate.*

___*Staying home with my new baby made me feel like I wasn't "doing" anything even though I had never worked that hard in my life.*

___*Sometimes, when I spend the day running errands, cleaning, carpooling, and making meals, I begin to think that anyone could do what I'm doing. ... I'm not so important.*

I Feel Like I Never Finish Anything!

Erma Bombeck likens the experience of motherhood to that of stringing beads. We go about our daily routines, stringing one brightly colored wooden knob after another, feeling pretty proud of ourselves. We assume we're accomplishing so much. But the illusion of productivity is shattered when, at the end of the day, we look down at the necklace only to discover that there is no knot. The once-strung beads are now scattered all over the place and we have to start all over.

Comedian Phyllis Diller quips, "Cleaning your house while your kids are still growing is like shoveling the walk before it stops snowing."[1] Other moms agree. Read their comments in the margin.

When do moms get to finish anything? We can't finish a meal without getting up and running to the stove, or the refrigerator, or to answer the phone. We scarcely finish a thought before somebody needs something and we've lost our concentration. What's more, finishing a sentence is a rare occurrence.

❀ What about you? Do unending tasks frustrate you?
How do you deal with the repetition?

_____

Picking up toys, doing laundry, making peanut butter and jelly sandwiches, and wiping off the kitchen counter... it's always there and I'm never done.

With preschoolers, it's difficult to do anything that lasts.

I can't even get the house clean. I get one room done and move on to the next, only to have the first room a disaster again.

After spending nine long, hard months awaiting my son's birth, I thought his arrival would be a relief. In some ways it was, but I was utterly unprepared for the difficulty of getting little sleep and still having so much to do. I never expected that caring for a newborn would be so all encompassing. And no matter how much I love my son, I still have a hard time functioning on so little sleep.

I'm a very organized person. I like everything in place. Before we had children, that's how things were. Now I look around and see all those toys —a huge mess— not made by me.

The job of mothering is unending. We know that we won't "complete" the assignment of raising our children until they're at least 18, and between infancy and 18 years is a loooooonnnnnggggg time. Even then, we continue to be Mom—for life.

I Feel So Exhausted All the Time!

Most babies don't sleep through the night in the first several months of life, and many others don't catch on for the entire first year or even longer! Once they finally settle into some kind of decent pattern, other challenges kick in—like disciplining a two-year-old, potty training, and answering questions, questions, questions. It's been said that life with a newborn is exhausting physically. And life with a toddler is exhausting mentally and emotionally.

❀ During your first few weeks or months of motherhood, estimate the number of hours you slept each night by circling one choice below:
less than four hours   *four to six hours*   *more than six hours*

I Feel So Out of Control!

Suddenly those who used to enjoy a sense of order in their days experience bedlam. How do you control your schedule when you realize your baby has an ear infection, or when he messes through his diaper just as you're ready to walk out the door for church, or when she trips and falls and everything comes to a screeching halt while you bandage a boo-boo? How do you maintain order in a home that formerly belonged to you but is now invaded by others who have stuff that never seems to stay in place? How do you go from the freedom of doing *what* you want *when* you want to a total lack of freedom?

Does mothering matter? It's a question that demands an answer. We live in a day when what you do equals who you are. A woman's worth is determined by the value of her work and the amount she accomplishes. And if your work is constantly unfinished or coming undone, is exhausting or without tangible reward, it is normal to question your worth. A mother of preschoolers asked: *"I wonder what I do that is worthwhile. I do chores—clean the house, do laundry, cook—and all of these are undone by the end of the day. I organize an event and no one even notices. How is my life going to count?"*

❀ How would you respond to her question? How does her life count?

_____

_____

Anne Morrow Lindbergh in her classic, *Gift from the Sea*, describes a woman's dilemma in this way:

> In the job of home-keeping there is no raise from the boss, and seldom praise from others to show us we have hit the mark. Except for the child, woman's creation is so often invisible, especially today. How can one point to this constant tangle of household chores, errands, and fragments of human relationships, as a creation? It is hard even to think of it as purposeful activity, so much of it is automatic. Woman herself begins to feel like a telephone exchange or a laundromat.[2]

One mother of young children, tired of feeling insignificant, decided to prove to her husband that what she did *mattered* by simply not doing it for one whole day. "What happened here today?" he asked when he walked into a kitchen strewed with dirty dishes, half-eaten sandwiches, and spilled cereal. Sitting on a couch amid the clutter of toys and newspapers, she replied, "You're always asking me what I do all day, so I decided not to do it."

What "They" Say About Mothering

Perhaps the need for significance is so great in the mother of young children be-cause she is surrounded on all sides by a culture that is itself confused about the value of mothering. In the past 50 years, opinions about a woman's worth and the value of motherhood have changed greatly.

In the '40s, women moved into the workplace to help out during World War II. In the '50s, they returned home to make the family the center of their attention. In the '60s, the Women's Movement blossomed, and in the '70s and '80s, women combined home and office. In the late '80s and early '90s, women realized they'd left something out in their pursuit of identity and began to explore the meaning of femininity in all its roles. Today, women work to make their families fit in with who they are—and who they are fit in with their families.

While the pendulum swings, mothers puzzle over the worth of their work. Some toil at mothering from dawn until dusk, with home as their sole place of vocation. Others who work outside the home delegate some maternal responsibilities to oth-ers for parts of the day or night. But all who mother face the challenge of investing time and energy in the lives of their children.

The world around us walls us in with two clear messages.

Mothering Is Not Viewed as a "Job."

If you mother, and only mother, society implies you don't work. And even if you mother while lawyering, wallpapering, or running a bookkeeping service from your home office, the mothering part of your day isn't valued as "work."

A while back, the state of California officially informed one mother who wanted to run for Congress that because mothers don't receive pay for their work, mothering was not recognized as an occupation on the ballot.

You won't find mothering listed on the employment résumés of most women, even though most women are mothers and have mothered for many years. And while it may be the work most faithfully completed, day in and day out, during the sum of a woman's life, you won't often see it mentioned in an obituary.

Mothering isn't viewed by our society as work. For that matter, neither is fathering. The task of raising and tending a family is not valued by our world. So it's pretty tough to value our major investment in life when the culture in which we live judges it as "unwork." By logical conclusion, what is "unwork" is leisure. Or optional. Or easy. In any case, it doesn't matter much. It's not significant and doesn't provide a person with a sense of worth.

Actually, motherhood requires more work than most of our "jobs." One mom describes the necessary qualifications this way: "Full-time motherhood requires the creativity of Thomas Edison, the diplomacy of Henry Kissinger, and the patience of Mother Teresa."[3] A MOPS group in Hamilton, New Zealand, wrote the following description, worded like a classified ad:

Situation Vacant—Housewife/Mother

Applications are invited for the position of manager to a lively team of four demanding individuals.

The successful applicant will be required to perform the following functions: companion, counselor, financial manager, buying officer, teacher, nurse, chef, nutritionist, decorator, cleaner, driver, childcare supervisor, social secretary, and recreation officer. Applicants must have unlimited energy and a strong sense of responsibility. They must be independent, self-motivated, and able to work in isolation without supervision, under stress, and adaptable enough to handle new developments in the life of the team, including emergencies and crises. They must be able to communicate with people of all ages, including teachers, doctors, business people, dentists, teenagers, and children. A good imagination, sensitivity, warmth, and an understanding of people is necessary.

HOURS—All waking moments and a 24-hour shift when necessary.

BENEFITS—No guaranteed holidays, no sick leave or maternity leave. No workers' compensation.

PAY—None. Allowances arranged from time to time with the income-earning member of the team. Successful applicant may be allowed/required to hold second job in addition to the one advertised here.

✿ Does the ad help you realize your value and abilities?
(circle)   *Yes*   *No*   *Somewhat*

✿ Write your own job description of mothering as it applies to your household. Be prepared to share your job description with other mothers at your group meeting.

_____

_____

_____

I need to know that what I'm doing has purpose and is important. I'll wait years before I see any results.

Mothering Is Not Valued as a Skill.

In today's culture, being a mother is similar to living at the low end of the food chain. As Joan France remarks in *Newsweek*, "This society neither respects nor rewards nurturing skills."[4] Take a look at the job vacancies today. Big gaps are growing in all service professions, with nursing and teaching experiencing gaping holes.

Mothering skills, where time and energy are invested in the lives of those who cannot do for themselves, are undervalued as well. One newspaper reported a woman, teeter-tottering in her decision to start a family, as saying: "My husband and I are trying to decide whether to get a dog or have a child. We haven't decided whether to ruin our carpets or to ruin our lives."

Sylvia Ann Hewlett, author of *When the Bough Breaks*, suggests that current legislation proves that nurturing skills are not valued. She asserts that most states give more attention to regulating dog kennels than day-care centers.

All around us are blatant messages that mothering is no more than an expensive hobby. Little praise or encouragement is given to those who invest their lives in the lives of children, trading personal fulfillment for the well-being of future adults.

I need affirmation that the choices I have made are worth it, especially when I cleaned the kitchen floor for the third time in a day or stayed home with a sick child.

✿ Place a checkmark in the boxes of the following qualities you possess already. Put a star by those qualities that are being developed in "on the job training":
- ☐ *The ability to work without supervision and with frequent distractions*
- ☐ *The ability to communicate well with people of all ages and education levels*
- ☐ *The ability to plan and coordinate the activities of several different people*
- ☐ *The ability to handle conflict with patience*[5]

Brenda Hunter, author of *Where Have All the Mothers Gone?* and *The Company of Women*, declares that "our culture tells mothers they are not that important in their children's lives. For three decades, mothering has been devalued in America. It has even become a status symbol for the modern woman to take as little time as possible away from work for full-time mothering."[6]

The message is strong. Mothering isn't viewed as a job nor valued as a skill. No wonder mothers wonder if mothering matters and question their significance.

❀ Wouldn't it be fun to know what your services would cost your family if they had to be done by an outside professional? Do some research to find out, such as calling a maid service, a caterer, a day care, a taxi company, etc. Share your findings with your group at your next meeting.

The Difference That Mothering Makes

"Honor your father and your mother, so that you may live long in the land the Lord your God is giving you."
Exodus 20:12

In order to truly see the difference that mothering makes, we must learn to redefine the worth of mothering. It is not defined by a paycheck or a promotion. The value of mothering is discovered in the peace of mind that comes from knowing you are doing all you can do with all you've been given. Indeed, mothering makes a difference in several areas.

Mothering Makes a Difference in the Life of Your Child.

In a moment when you wonder whether you matter to your children, read this:

Everybody knows that a good mother gives her children a feeling of trust and stability. She is the one they can count on for the things that matter most of all. She is their food and their bed and their extra blanket when it grows cold in the night; she is their warmth and health and their shelter; she is the one they want to be near when they cry. She is the only person in the whole world, or in a whole lifetime, who can be these things to her children. There is no substitute for her. Somehow even her clothes feel different to her children's hands from anybody else's clothes. Only to touch her skirt or her sleeve makes a troubled child feel better.[7]

—*The Little Locksmith*
Katherine Butler Hathaway

You are the mother your child needs. God has chosen you for the job. No one else in the world can mean as much to your child as you.

1. *You make a difference in the physical development of your child.*
   Early childhood is a critical time. In fact, according to new scientific evidence, these fleeting years are even more crucial than we once realized. Reports now tell us that a child's environment from birth to age three helps determine brain structure and ability to learn.

A 1994 Carnegie Corporation report states:

- Brain development before age one is more rapid and extensive, more vulnerable to environmental influence, and longer-lasting than previously realized;
- The environment affects the number of brain cells, connections among them, and the way connections are wired;
- Early stress has a negative impact on brain development.

This three-year study concludes that millions of infants and toddlers are so deprived of medical care, loving support, and intellectual stimulation that their growth into healthy adulthood is threatened.[8] Your mothering matters to the physical development of your child.

*We must remember that there is no one-to-one correlation between
the mother and a child's physical imperfections, illnesses, diseases, learning problems,
or birth defects. God has made each person unique and special.
God's presence is often most clearly felt in the life of a special needs child.*

❀ As we consider our role in the physical development of our children, what message of encouragement could you send the mother of a special needs child?

_____

_____

2. *You make a difference in the emotional development of your child.*
   Your child's ability to learn as well as her ability to love is influenced at this early age. A mother's nurturing love builds the foundation of the child's ability to love others, to learn, and to adjust to his or her environment.

   Speaking at the 1994 MOPS International Leadership Convention, child expert and author Jeanne Hendricks said: "To the newborn child, people are everything. The earliest social skill is when that little infant can find and hold the eyes of an adult in what we call the 'quiet-alert' stage. And you never forget it once you've experienced it. It's when that little one looks at you and says, 'Can I trust you?' Because the first developmental task of a newborn child is to find out, 'Is this a safe world? Am I going to be accepted and loved?'"

   Along similar lines, other child-development experts tell us that secure attachment with the mother forms the foundation for the child's entire self-structure and identity. A parent and child work together to create an individual who can

"May she who gave you birth rejoice!"
Proverbs 23:25

look in a mirror and squeal with delight, "That's me!" According to Assistant Professor of Psychology at the University of Colorado, Sandra Pipp: "Infants who are securely attached to their mothers and fathers have a more complex knowledge of themselves and others than insecurely attached infants. Children from one to three years of age who are more securely attached are able to relate to themselves and their parents in more ways than those who are insecurely attached."[9]

Writing one hundred years ago, Sigmund Freud described the relationship of a young child to his mother as "unique, without parallel, established unalterably for a whole lifetime as the first and strongest love object and as the prototype of all later love relationships for both sexes."[10] Even earlier, these words appeared in *Plato's Republic*: "You know that the beginning is the most important part of any work, especially in the care of a young and tender thing; for that is the time at which the character is being formed and the desired impression is more readily taken."

The mother not only feeds the physical being but also the emotional self and soul of the child. When we downplay the contribution of the mother in the life of a child, especially in the early years, we simply ignore her vital role in that child's development. Dr. Marianne Neifert, known to millions as "Dr. Mom," looks back at her own inadequate presence for bonding in the lives of some of her children and boldly asserts: "There is something terribly abnormal about separating mothers from their babies. We must stop glamorizing it. ... A baby has some rights to her mother."[11]

❋ Mothers who worry about bonding with their infants usually have little reason for concern. Check the following bonding activities you routinely perform(ed). Add to the list other things you do.

☐ smile ☐ sing ☐ feed ☐ pick up your infant
☐ laugh ☐ coo ☐ comfort ☐ change the diaper/clothing
☐ touch ☐ cuddle ☐ talk to your infant ☐ introduce new objects
☐ other _____

Mothering Makes a Difference in the Life of the Mother.

Bit by bit, the impact of our lives on those of our children becomes clearer.

In the adjustment to becoming a mother, we often don't understand the difference our efforts make. But bit by bit, the impact of our lives on those of our children becomes clearer.

Does it matter if a mother rolls over and goes back to sleep, ignoring her three-month-old who wakes at two o'clock in the morning? Does it matter if a mother sits on the front porch and watches her toddler follow a ball into the busy street, without running to stop him at the curb? Does it matter if a mother ignores another straight-A report card from her perfectionist 11-year-old daughter because, after all, she always makes straight As? Does it matter if a mother obeys the closed door rule of silence imposed on her by a teenage son in whose drawer she has found what looks like cocaine?

Mothering matters. And if we invest ourselves in the formative years when a child is dependent upon parents for his or her development, we will reap the benefits later in life with the joy of living with a more secure and independent child.

In her address to the 1990 graduating class of Wellesley College, this line drew then-First Lady Barbara Bush the most fervent applause: "At the end of your life, you'll never regret not having passed one more test, not winning one more verdict, or not closing one more deal. You will regret times not spent with a husband, a friend, a child, or a parent."

The next time you're tempted to think you aren't worth very much or that what you're doing as a mother isn't important, consider the following:

You Are a Key Person.

Xvxn though my typxwritxr is an old modxl, it works vxry wxll xxcxpt for onx kxy. You would think that with all thx othxr kxys functioning propxrly, onx kxy not working would hardly bx noticxd, but just onx kxy out of whack sxxms to ruin thx wholx xffort.

You may say to yoursxlf, "Wxll, I'm only onx pxrson, no onx will xvxn noticx if I don't quitx do my bxst."

But it doxs makx a diffxrxncx bxcausx to bx xffxctivx an organization nxxds activx participation by xvxryonx to the bxst of his and hxr ability.

So thx nxxt timx you think you arx not important, rxmxmbxr my old typxwritxr.

You arx a kxy pxrson![12]

The next time you feel insignificant, "x" yourself out of the picture. What's wrong with that picture? "X" yourself out of Christmas preparations or just-wake-up-in-the-morning times, and what is missing? You are a key person. You are the mother of your children because God has chosen you for them.

> You are the mother of your children because God has chosen you for them.

Mothering Makes a Difference in the World.

At MOPS International, we're fond of the motto that mothering matters ... because "today makes a difference tomorrow." We've become accustomed to applying that sentiment to the maintenance of our planet. Most of us have become knowledgeable and skilled at recycling plastic milk bottles and glass jelly jars. Empty aluminum cans fill bags in garages to be exchanged for pennies at the grocery store. There are even those among us who reuse shopping bags and have converted our toilets with water-saving devices.

We would be wise to transfer this truth—that today makes a difference tomorrow—to our mothering. In a speech to MOPS leaders, Jeanne Hendricks warned that we are more concerned about making a better world for our children than we are about making better children for our world. Mothering matters not only to the child and to the mother, but also to the world in which we live.

🌸 Reread *This Week's Verse* on page 9. Underline the portion of the verse that explains the long-term effect of mothering. Practice saying the verse until you can recite it from memory.

🌸 Check the activities you do or plan to do to make better children for our world.
   ☐ *Read to them from the Bible.*　　☐ *Discipline them.*
   ☐ *Read Bible-based storybooks.*　　☐ *Attend church together.*
   ☐ *Pray with them and for them.*　　☐ *Other_____*

God Values Mothers.

Of the infinite number of creative possibilities, God chose the model of families where children are born and nurtured and where mothers play a key role. Review the different circumstances of these Bible mothers: Eve (Gen. 4); Sarah (Gen. 16—18); Hannah (1 Sam. 1), and Elizabeth (Luke 1).

🌿 Do you think any of these women ever questioned their value as mothers? *(circle)*　　　Yes　　　No

🌿 How does God value these and all mothers? Place a dot on the seesaw to indicate your opinion.

very much　　　　　　　　　　　*some*　　　　　　　　　*not very much*

🌸 What is your response to the question: "Does mothering matter?" Take a minute to write your feelings. Refer to this week's *Mothering Maxim.* Be prepared to share your response with your group.

_____

_____

Week 2

Identity

Sometimes I'm Not Sure Who I Am

She shifted the weight of the infant seat to one hip and used it to prop open the door to the hair salon as her three-year-old passed through. "Whew! I made it!" Cheryl told the receptionist with a laugh. "And only five minutes late!"

The receptionist smiled and led Cheryl, Bryan, and baby Allison back to Patti, who greeted the gang with gusto. "Hey, Bryan! Here's a special spot for you. You can entertain your little sister while I cut your mom's hair. Okay, buddy?"

"I'm so glad to be here," Cheryl told Patti. "My hair has been driving me nuts. I only hope the kids will hold up for the next 15 minutes."

"They'll be fine," Patti assured her. "You've got such great kids," she added as she laid Cheryl back in the chair to wash her hair.

As Patti lathered her head, the compliment oozed into Cheryl's tired muscles like a soothing ointment. They *were* good kids, and she loved them more than life itself.

Rinsed and toweled, Cheryl stepped over some toys to the styling chair where Patti clipped on an apron and then was called to the telephone. "I'll be back in a sec," she said, spinning Cheryl around to face the mirror.

Ugh! she thought. *I should have put on some makeup. But there wasn't time. There never is anymore.* With her wet hair slicked back from her face, she could see new creases in her forehead. She hardly recognized herself. *Is this what I look like now?* Cheryl wondered.

Then suddenly, surprisingly, she felt a weird chill as she saw staring back at her not just a tired mom or an older version of herself—but someone else, someone who

This Week's Verse
"Therefore, if anyone is in Christ, he is a new creation; the old has gone, the new has come."
2 Corinthians 5:17

Mothering Maxim
To know me—who I am and who I am not—is to love me.

21

Who am I? Ha!
That's easy, right?
I'm a mom. I'm a wife.
I'm a need-meeter.
I'm a cook.
I'm a milk-machine.
I'm a laundromat.
I'm tired.
I'm . . . not sure
anymore.

looked familiar and yet couldn't be identified. She peered closer. It wasn't so much any particular feature, but the expression, the whole package. And then she knew. Staring back at her from the reflection in the mirror was the face of her mother.

She drew in her breath quickly. *Who are you?* she wondered to the face in the mirror. *Who am I anymore?*

❀ How would you answer the question, "Who am I?" Jot down your initial response.

_____

_____

I'm Not Sure Who I Am

Whether we're 12 or 20, 32 or 47, we keep asking ourselves: "Who am I?" In some stages of life, we embrace the question willingly and engage in a mental wrestling match until we reach a satisfying answer. But for the mother of young children, the question can seem a bit threatening. All tangled up with our roles and responsibilities, the answer is elusive.

I didn't know
I'd have to give up
so much of myself.
I'm about 99 percent
mom and only
1 percent myself.

As mothers, we need to redefine ourselves. We need to find and accept the kind of definition that will sustain us during this season when we are pulled and stretched and drained and sometimes overwhelmed by the responsibility of taking care of others. Though most of us enjoy what we're doing, we're like Cheryl who was suddenly confronted with the question that all new mothers inevitably ask: "Who am I *now?*"

❀ How well do you know yourself? What three adjectives or phrases best describe you?

1. _____

2. _____

3. _____

Learn to be your own best friend by learning how to love, affirm, and encourage yourself. On your own paper, write a complimentary description or sentence and tape it to your bathroom mirror. Keep it there through the remainder of this week. In your group, be prepared to discuss the difference between pride and self-worth.

Who Am I?

A mother tends to define herself most easily in terms of her external circumstances. She looks in the mirror and, instead of an identity in its own right, she sees the various facets of her life staring back at her.

One mom expressed the feeling as a fear that she would lose her identity to all the roles she fulfilled in a 24-hour-a-day 7-day-a-week responsibility. Read it in the margin.

This mom thing has really shaken me to the core. I don't have a clue who I am—even after five personality tests. There's a looming feeling that if I don't figure it out soon, I'm going to ruin three young lives.

I Am What I Do.

When she goes to a school event or sits next to a stranger in church who asks, "What do you do?" a woman is likely to label herself in terms of a relationship or a job description—"I'm Beth's mom"; "I'm Tom's wife"; "I'm an accountant"; "I'm a part-time consultant."

For moms who stay home with their children, this common ice-breaker often causes them to cringe: *I make a new friend who hands me her business card and then asks me what I do, and I don't know what to say.*

One stay-at-home mom attended a fancy dinner party with her husband. As they mingled with many of his clients, she heard people defining themselves with important job titles. So she armed herself with a powerful answer. Sure enough, someone finally asked her: "And what do *you* do?"

"I'm the CEO of my family!" she shot back proudly.

✿ If you are a stay-at-home mom, create a business card with your name, job title, business address, phone, and a motto or slogan. Design a logo if you have artistic ability. Be prepared to show your business card to your group at the next meeting.

I Am What Others Need Me To Be.

I'm surprised that I'm so consumed by my children and their needs.

My baby began to control my life even before she was born, directing me from the womb with demands like: "Eat now! Rest more! Drink more water! Don't eat that!"

My baby takes up all of my day— and all of myself.

This season of life is a season of self-sacrifice, but as moms, we often lose our identities in the overwhelming desire or sense of responsibility to be a need-meeter. It's as if we cease to exist for anything other than meeting the needs of others, and we not only begin to identify ourselves in that way, but we begin to measure our value and worth by our ability to meet those needs. If my baby is good (sleeps through the night, learns to crawl or walk on schedule, interacts well with other children), then I tell myself that I have met his needs and I am good. If my baby acts badly (screams when I leave the room, hits other children, or flushes my watch down the toilet), then I accuse myself of not meeting her needs and I am bad.

Meeting the needs of her husband can also preempt a mom's own identity. She is the one who listens to his dreams. She is the source of his inspirations and passion. She is the caretaker who makes sure he has clean shirts and socks. She advises him in his interactions with the children as well as those he has with their couple-friends. Therefore, when he succeeds, she succeeds. When he fails, she fails. What he thinks becomes what she thinks. Her identity can become an extension of his.

While this may sound like an oversimplification, we often do get our identities confused with the role of need-meeter.

Remember, this is a book about finding balance in your life. On the seesaw scale below, put an X to identify where you are:

consumed with needs of family   *consumed with self*

I Am What I Accomplish.

As stated in the last chapter on significance, many of us believe that who we are equals what we accomplish. "I'm a painter; here are my pictures." Or, "I'm an accountant; here is my Rolodex of clients." We are validated by the results of our efforts. In a stage of life where we may accomplish little more than getting to the grocery store or keeping up with the dirty dishes and diapers, an identity based on accomplishment is an identity at risk.

Where do you see yourself on the opposite poles of being versus doing? On the seesaw below, put an X to identify where you are.

I focus on the "being" aspect of me.   *I focus on the "doing" aspect of me.*

I Am What I've Experienced.

Another partial picture of identity is taken from the past. From the time we feed as infants in our mother's arms and focus on her eyes, only inches from our own, we are drinking in messages about who we are. She becomes the mirror that gives us our identity. In her praise and criticism, patience and impatience, approval and disapproval, we develop an image of who we are.

So, too, with our father. He comes home from work and lifts us in the air, mirroring back to us how important we are to him. Or, he brushes us aside to concentrate on the newspaper, and we conclude that we are of no value at all.

Siblings and our birth order among them in the family describe our place in the scheme of life. As firstborns, we often see a reflection of superiority in our first-place rankings. As second-borns, we see competition and conditional love in the eyes of the one above us. Opposite-sex siblings challenge our sexual identity while same-sex siblings underline it.

And those of us who experienced some trauma in our past often live with wounded identities in the present. The painful past scatters the shards of broken images, leaving us unsure of who we were, who we are, and who we will become.

✿ Some of us get bogged down in negative messages from the past and need more help than a husband or relative can offer. Here are some warning signs that—if they persist—might mean you should turn to a pastor or professional counselor for help. Check any that have characterized you for at least three weeks:

☐ loss of pleasure in life ☐ nervousness
☐ difficulty concentrating ☐ feeling of worthlessness or guilt
☐ change in weight ☐ low energy
☐ sleeplessness ☐ change in appetite

Who Am I *Not?*

While the mirrors around us reflect an incomplete picture of identity, they can also offer inaccurate reflections, confusing our understanding of who we are. Gregg Lewis observes, "Often the picture we get of ourselves from the outside world is as distorted as the bizarre reflection you might see in a House of Mirrors at a county fair."[1]

To understand who we are, we have to come to grips with who we are not.

I Am Not My Children.

I feel strange now
when I go out without
the kids {which is rare}
. . . like I'm not
as important alone.

In this all-consuming,
new role of mothering,
I fear that I've lost me.
I live through
my children. My self-
esteem is going!

In this season of constant giving, when our children are nearly totally dependent upon us, we derive some sense of value from their responses and accomplishments, but the lines separating us can grow fuzzy. We have to remind ourselves that we are separate. The goal of our role as mothers, in fact, is to continually strengthen that separateness. As psychologist Erik Fromm writes, "In motherly love, two people who were one become separate."[2]

I Am Not My Mother.

Perhaps one of the greatest shocks of mothering is looking at ourselves and seeing the traits of our own mothers: "In giving birth, a woman suddenly confronts her parenting history. She reflects on her early childhood as she cares for her baby. Moreover, a woman identifies with her own mother when she becomes a mother for the first time."[3]

Mothers of young children must process this stage of identity development. Yes, each of us possesses some of the qualities of our own mothers. But, at the same time, each of us is unique. A pivotal truth is that "similar to" does not mean "the same as." While you may have inherited your mother's bone structure, you do not necessarily have her temper. While you may have picked up a creative streak from her, you don't have to repeat her habit of negative nagging.

You may be like your mother in some ways, but you are not your mother. Nor are you your mother-in-law, your grandmother, or your stepmother.

I Am Not My Sister, My Neighbor, or Any Other Woman.

Sure, your older sister has this mothering thing down pat. She's been at it for eight years longer than you have. And your supermom neighbor probably just *looks* like she knows what she's doing. But I'll bet that beneath her well-applied makeup and well-maintained house, she still struggles with some aspect of her day. Don't let her fool you.

To "compare" means to examine characteristics and qualities in order to determine differences and similarities. That's healthy; we can all improve on certain qualities and skills. But when we use comparisons to determine our personal worth, we're looking in the wrong direction. Your value is not dependent upon how you stack up next to someone else. You are not your sister, your neighbor, or anyone else you admire.

✿ In what ways are you one-of-a-kind in your family line?

physical feature _____

talent/ability _____

interest/hobby _____

So Who Am I Really?

If you're more than the sum of your responsibilities and relationships, your accomplishments and your past, and you know who you are not, then who are you, really? The question still begs an answer, and the truth is simpler, greater, and more enduring than all these partial or inaccurate reflections.

Our true identity comes not from looking into horizontal mirrors—at reflections of ourselves or our mothers or our past—but looking up at God. As we gaze into His face, we begin to get a true picture of ourselves. He created us in His image.

In his book, *Life Mapping,* John Trent puts it this way:

Did you know that there's a miraculous mirror you can go to anytime that will reflect the brightest and best part of you? It's a mirror not of make-believe ... but one of rock-solid reality. Just open your Bible to 2 Corinthians 3:18 and you'll find a mirror that can reveal your strengths and point you toward the person you'd most like to become.[4]

☘ Read 2 Corinthians 3:18 in the margin. Beneath the verse write the name of the person we are to most resemble.

In his book, *The Sensation of Being Somebody,* Maurice Wagner suggests that all images bear some relationship to the object they represent. In other words, God created us to represent Him; He put His thumbprint upon our beings, and through our relationship with Him, we begin to know and understand and accept ourselves. For some, this is a challenging process.

☘ Read Genesis 1:26-27,31 in your Bible. If you were to see yourself as God sees you, how would your opinion of yourself be different?

_____
_____

"And we, who with unveiled faces all reflect the Lord's glory, are being transformed into his likeness with ever-increasing glory, which comes from the Lord, who is the Spirit."

2 Corinthians 3:18

The goal is to know our true identity in God's eyes because the Bible promises that Truth—found in the person of Jesus Christ—will set us free (see John 8:32). The Bible gives us three foundational truths that tell us who we are. As you read them, consider how they apply to you.

I Am Unique.

God creates each of us as a unique being. You are you—a combination of personality traits, physical makeup, talents, and abilities. You are either an extrovert or an introvert, a morning or night person, type A or B on the stress scale, small- or large-boned; the list could go on. Others may have similar traits, but no one is packaged exactly like you. God has created you uniquely ... to be who you are.

Need scientific proof? Law enforcement experts have long used the technique of identifying people by means of their fingerprints because no two are the same. Today, research in DNA reveals that the smallest of body parts (hair samples or skin flakes, for example) can identify individuals with equal accuracy.

Mothers are quick to recognize the uniqueness of their children. No two siblings are exactly alike. Though both are brought up in the same environment, one may be strong-willed while the other is compliant. One loves all foods; the other is picky. Yet are you as quick to acknowledge and accept your own uniqueness? Each of you represents a unique combination of heredity and environment that, woven together, forms the framework of who you are, created in God's image, for His unique purpose. You are unique.

I Am Imperfect.

What surprises me most about being a mother is myself. My temper and impatience with my kids.

Each of us, no matter how hard we try, falls short of perfection, and this imperfection is most often revealed within the context of our close relationships. We try to be good mothers, but sometimes what we see surprises—and disappoints—us.

The comforting truth is that God knows about our imperfections. In fact, that's the reason He sent His Son, Jesus, to die on the cross—to forgive us for our "imperfectness." Living in the reality of that, forgiveness gives us the strength to keep going, to forgive ourselves, and to accept ourselves.

"Indeed, the struggle of self-acceptance is, in a strong sense, a case of disillusionment," writes Martha Thatcher. "We may be disappointed in our character, our abilities, or our role in life; we had thought it would all be quite different. No matter how many good points about ourselves we become aware of, we are still disappointed in what is not there."[5]

Coming to grips with who we are doesn't mean that we wallow in our imperfections. We don't have to replay negative messages over and over in our minds, brainwashing ourselves about what we lack in order to know ourselves. But coming to see ourselves in truth requires that we take off any masks of denial and admit our inadequacies. They, too, help us define ourselves.

In his book, *The Art of Learning to Love Yourself*, Cecil Osborne writes, "The people I know who truly like themselves as persons, apart from their roles in life as husband, wife, parent, or job-holder, are those who have learned to be honest with themselves and who to some degree understand themselves."[6]

You are imperfect. You are fallible human beings who are in process. You will make mistakes; you will lose your patience; you will sometimes act unlovingly.

I Am Loved.

God loves us unconditionally—without regard to our performance or goodness or consistent ability to be good mothers. One of the best-known verses of the Bible is John 3:16. Read it in the margin.

Substitute your own name for *the world* in this verse, and you'll have a true message of God's love for you. In simplest terms, God assures us that we are loved. Each one of us. In fact, we are so very loved that God Himself died for us on the cross.

So whether or not your mother loved you, your child tells you you're special, or your husband says it often enough, the truth is, you are loved.

> "For God so loved the world that he gave his one and only Son, that whoever believes in him shall not perish but have eternal life." John 3:16

When asked what moms need most, many said "acceptance." Answer the following questions by checking your response:

Do you accept yourself?	☐ *Yes*	☐ *No*
Do you believe that God accepts you?	☐ *Yes*	☐ *No*
Does God really love you?	☐ *Yes*	☐ *No*

If you do not have a genuine love relationship with God, read John 3:16 printed in the margin. This verse tells you that God gave His only Son, Jesus Christ, as payment for your sins. Jesus' death removed the penalty of death and replaced it with eternal life. If you want to receive Jesus as your personal Savior and take Him as Lord of your life, talk to Him in prayer.

Confess that you are a sinner in need of a Savior (see Rom. 6:23). Turn away from your sins (repent) and ask Christ to forgive you for living apart from Him. Invite Christ to be your Savior right now. Surrender your will to Him as Lord of your life.

Thank God for your salvation and new eternal life in Christ! Read 2 Corinthians 5:17, This Week's Verse, printed on page 21. Then tell a Christian friend or your group leader about your decision!

Getting to Know Me

Learning to apply these truths in our lives as mothers of young children is a process. In a simple checklist, here's what these truths mean:

We Need to Know Ourselves the Way God Knows Us.

If we know ourselves—recognizing our uniqueness and our imperfections—and know that God loves us, we are free to accept ourselves. We are even free to love ourselves. God tells us to love our neighbors as *ourselves* (see Matt. 22:39). This is not a prideful type of self-love but a secure acceptance of ourselves. It is seeing ourselves as God sees us—our true identity—which sets us free from guilt, self-consciousness, and put-downs. Self-acceptance meets a critical need that moms have.

❀ Read the following statements about God's love for you. In the margin, put a star by those you feel to be true and a question mark if there are statements you have difficulty accepting. Over the next few days, pray about the question marks. Ask God to show you His love in these ways.

Because God loves me ...

- *He is slow to lose patience with me.*
- *He takes the circumstances of my life and uses them in a constructive way for my growth.*
- *He does not treat me as an object to be possessed and manipulated.*
- *He has no need to impress me with how great and powerful He is because He is God, nor does He belittle me as His child to show me how important He is.*
- *He is for me. He wants to see me mature and develop in His love.*
- *He does not send down His wrath on every little mistake I make, of which there are many.*
- *He does not keep score of all my sins and then beat me over the head with them whenever He gets the chance.*
- *He is deeply grieved when I do not walk in the ways that please Him because He sees this as evidence that I don't trust Him and love Him as I should.*
- *He rejoices when I experience His power and strength and stand up under the pressures of life for His Name's sake.*
- *He keeps on working patiently with me even when I feel like giving up and can't see why He doesn't give up with me, too.*
- *He keeps on trusting me when at times I don't even trust myself.*
- *He never says, "There is no hope for you." Rather, He patiently works with me, loves me, and disciplines me in such a way that it is hard for me to understand the depth of His concern for me.*
- *He never forsakes me even though many of my friends might.*[7]

We Need to Care for Ourselves for the Sake of Our Children.

Author and mother Valerie Bell exhorts: "Becoming a parent should motivate moms and dads to care for themselves emotionally. Sometimes we meet our children's needs by meeting our own needs. It seems like a paradox, but it's true. *Take care of your emotional health for the sake of your child.* If you love your child, you should be willing to do any preventive work that keeps you from passing on your own problems to your child. And along the way, you will be doing yourself an enormous favor as well."[8]

Valerie Bell goes on to say: "It's hard for a child to trust an adult who is like an emotional yo-yo—loving one minute, angry and explosive the next. An unpredictable parent, one given to wide emotional swings, is an unstable parent."[9]

We Need to Accept Ourselves for the Sake of Others Around Us.

As stated, the Golden Rule tells us to love our neighbor as ourselves. The very core of the rule requires that we love ourselves. For if, in fact, we do not love ourselves, we are unable to truly love others.

♣ Reread this week's *Mothering Maxim* on page 21. If you can affirm this statement, underline it. If not, explain why in the margin.

Self-Discovery

In his book, *That Incredible Christian*, A. W. Tozer reminds us that God already knows us thoroughly (see Ps. 139:1-6). However, we need to know ourselves. Tozer offers some rules for self-discovery. He says we may be known by the following:

- *What we want most. ... Ask your heart: What would you rather have than anything else in the world? Reject the conventional answer. Insist on the true one, and when you have heard it, you will know the kind of person you are.*

- *What we think about most. ... Our thoughts will cluster about our secret heart treasure, and whatever that is will reveal what we are. "Where your treasure is, there will your heart be also."*

- *How we use our money. ... We must pay taxes and provide the necessities of life for ourselves and family. That is routine and tells us little about ourselves. But whatever money is left to do with as we please—that will tell us a great deal indeed.*

- *What we do with our leisure time. A large share of our time is already spoken for ... but we do have some free time. What we do with it is vital. Most people waste it. ... What I do with mine reveals the kind of person I am.*

- *The company we enjoy. There is a law of moral attraction that draws every person to the society most like their self. "Being let go, they went to their own company." Where we go when we are free to go where we will is a near infallible index of character.*

Though I love my children and am proud of them, their accomplishments are not my report card, nor their shortfalls my failure. I can't wrap my ego around them.

I'm not who I thought I was. I've been operating from behind masks of who I wanted to be most of my teenage and adult years. But now God is holding a mirror before me, helping me see who I really am.

- *Whom we admire. ... We can learn the true state of our minds by examining our un-expressed admirations. Israel often admired ... the pagan nations around them, and so forgot the law and the promises and the fathers. ...*[10]

❀ Now describe yourself using Tozer's rules of self-discovery.

What I think about most _____

What I want most _____

How I use my money _____

How I use my leisure time _____

The company I enjoy _____

Whom I admire _____

"O Lord, you have searched me and you know me. You know when I sit and when I rise; you perceive my thoughts from afar. You discern my going out and my lying down; you are familiar with all my ways."
Psalm 139:1-2

Who am I? The question keeps popping up as we grow and change. Which mirror gives the truest answer, the one that will sustain us through changing circumstances and changing roles? Horizontal mirrors will help you to know parts of yourself as you look to your families and your past for answers. But it is the vertical mirror—gazing at God—that provides the truest reflections of yourself. God reminds you who you are. He tells you the truth that sets you free to know yourself, to accept yourself, and therefore to be yourself.

❀ Repeat this prayer of acceptance:
Today, O Lord, I accept Your acceptance of me.
I confess that You are always with me and always for me.
I receive into my spirit Your grace, Your mercy, Your care.
I rest in Your love, O Lord, I rest in Your love. Amen.[11]

Week Three

Growth

Sometimes I Long to Develop Who I Am

Sheila closed the baby's door and tiptoed down the hall toward the kitchen. The muscles in the back of her neck felt tense. She raised her hand to massage them as she thought about her choices.

She had an hour. Maybe an hour and a half. Amanda had been invited to a friend's home after preschool; after an active morning, Josh should sleep awhile. At 13 months, he was into everything. Just this morning, he'd committed his own version of "breaking and entering." Somehow he'd negotiated the childproof knob on the pantry and sprinkled a package of rice all over the pantry shelves and the kitchen floor.

Don't think about that now, Sheila scolded herself. *You've only got an hour, so use it.*

What she really wanted to do was to play the piano. Sheila had been a piano major in college and had taught high school music before Amanda was born. Even after Amanda's birth—for a couple of years, at least—she'd been able to squeeze in a few neighborhood piano lessons during afternoon nap time. These days she barely had time to sit down at all.

Chopin called to her from the upright piano in the family room. Favorite nocturnes played through her head, and she entered into a familiar tug-of-war. There was a load of wash to do, and she really should start dinner—a process much easier without Josh around.

Brahms beckoned her. She wavered. No! This was not the time to succumb. She needed to make out a grocery list ... and change the kitty litter—another impossible task with Josh "helping."

This Week's Verse
"He who began a good work in you will carry it on to completion until the day of Christ Jesus." Philippians 1:6

Mothering Maxim
What I am is God's gift to me. What I become is my gift to God.

As she passed the piano, however, Mozart moved her to sit down. *Well, just a few minutes*, she rationalized. She touched the ivory keys, immediately becoming lost in the music.

She knew she should be playing like this every day! Otherwise, she'd lose her touch. Oh, how she longed for the freedom she once had to play and play and play. She had dreamed of obtaining a faculty position at the junior college in town. Could that dream still come true?

For 15 whole minutes she played, building toward a loud crescendo. Then she heard Josh's cries echoing down the hall. Actually, they were wails. Her playing had awakened him.

How stupid of me, she thought as she slammed the cover down on the keyboard and headed down the hall. *Now I'll never get anything done this afternoon! I shouldn't have played the piano.*

♣ What do you think? Was Sheila "stupid" to play the piano when other tasks needed to be done? Write your opinion here:

_____

_____

_____

Life Lived on Hold

Before I had children I spent a lot of time doing needlework. After my second was born, I had to force myself to finish his birth sampler. I felt my creative side was being drowned in a sea of practicality.

In this season of life, moms often make time for everyone and everything except themselves. We tend to assume that babies, toddlers, and husbands can't wait for attention—but *we* can. So we put our dreams and personal development on hold. And sometimes we get stuck in the distraction of the demands made upon us.

Some moms describe this feeling of being stuck as "mind mush." Where once we may have carried on intellectually stimulating dialogues, we now feel that our brains are turning to mush. We even fear we may lose the ability to think altogether!

Others get stuck in the midst of constant baby talk, which can be embarrassing when it slips out in adult company. Some moms expressed their frustration this way: *I never get to finish a sentence, so I rarely speak in full sentences anymore. All I talk about these days is potty-this and potty-that. I forget how to talk in grown-up language. The other day I told a girlfriend to look at the moo-moos.*

✿ Preschoolers eventually have to give up baby talk. In the margin, jot some words or phrases you can begin working on with your child(ren) to replace with grown-up language.

Some mothers bemoan the "shelving" of parts of their personhood. Mothers of preschoolers need significance, to know that their doing—their mothering—matters. They also need a sense of identity—to know who they are and to be that person with confidence.

The Need to Grow

The third need we experience as mothers of young children is the need to grow and develop ourselves, both in what we do and in who we are. We have a built-in longing for self-improvement—whether that means nurturing a dream or developing more patience. Though we enjoy investing ourselves in our families, we periodically yearn to reach and change and try and experiment and experience other parts of our being. To paint! To read! To think! To create! To converse! Ah ... to dream!

✿ Check the statements that describe something you'd like to do:

- ☐ Become a professional photographer.
- ☐ Raise golden retrievers.
- ☐ Be an Olympic medalist.
- ☐ Start a cake decoration business at home.
- ☐ Be a clown at children's birthday parties.
- ☐ Master the computer.

- ☐ Design clothes.
- ☐ Open a boutique.
- ☐ Write a book.
- ☐ Play the piano.
- ☐ Arrange flowers.

- ☐ List your own possibilities: _____

My husband asked what my hobbies were and I couldn't give him an answer, other than being a mom and wife. I laid everything aside when we had our daughter.

Season of Self-Sacrifice

Mothering, by its very nature, requires self-sacrifice. This is a season when self-fulfillment naturally conflicts with self-sacrifice. Besides, we all know that, out of necessity, self-sacrifice usually wins. For most, this process begins with pregnancy when the comfort and shape of the body are compromised. Emotions spin out of control. Feet swell. Abdomens distend. Blood pressure increases.

And then at last—D-day—when the mother gives up her modesty as the baby squeezes through the birth canal, a passageway 10 times smaller than it seems it should be. One woman described delivery as the process of pushing a bowling ball out one nostril. Another said it is like taking your lower lip and stretching it up over your forehead.

For those who have become mothers through adoption, the sacrifice is of the heart rather than the body. Waiting for a child can be lengthy and unpredictable. And then there is the disappointment of not being part of the birth process.

While mothering young children, we learn plenty about giving up time and sleep. As we bathe wobbly, wrinkly babies, spoon sloppy cereal into mouths more interested in making bubbles, train resistant toddlers in the meaning of the word *no*, patiently watch chubby fingers master shoelaces, and guide them as they learn to print the letters of their names—we come to know that mothering well means investing in the lives of people other than ourselves.

Love is expensive. And our children are well-served by mothers who are willing to give—and give *up*—freely. But mothering well shouldn't and doesn't require us to shelve our personal needs completely. Moms, too, have a legitimate need to grow as individuals, to develop their talents and abilities (doing) as well as to strengthen their characters (being).

Growth can't wait until the empty nest. Here are some reasons why:

You Need to Develop Yourself.

Today represents an important season in your life. You can't skip it or ignore it. And you can't ignore or neglect yourself during this season or you may find a gaping hole in the next.

You probably have dreams and desires that need to be expressed. You may have creative juices that require an outlet of expression. The "you" that has been growing since your own birth doesn't cease to exist because you've given birth to another.

❀ Make a "dreamcatcher." Dreamcatchers are tangible symbols that remind us of those things we hold dear or give us targets at which to aim.
1. A seashell, a smooth rock from a mountain stream, a refrigerator magnet of an artist's easel and brush, or a writer's quill may serve as reminders to keep your dream alive and growing. List some symbols that have meaning to you.

_____

2. Select a spot to display reminders, such as a place on your nightstand, a bookshelf, or a space on the refrigerator door.
3. Be on the lookout for symbols to add to your collection. Periodically pause to enjoy them and to remind yourself of the growth choices in your life—the embers of dreams that in the future you know will be kindled into flames.

I knew I wanted to be a mother and take that job seriously. But at the same time, I knew I had to cultivate my own potential in areas outside of mothering.

I need to know my individuality has not been totally sacrificed to be a mother.

Your Family Needs You to Develop Yourself.

Every member of your family will benefit from the you that you are becoming. Your family will also benefit from the wholeness of your example. They need the challenge and inspiration of your growth in order to grow themselves.

While at times it might seem that investing in yourself is an abandonment of others in your life, the truth is that when you invest in your own growth, you are more able to influence the growth of those around you. They learn to take care of themselves as they see you balancing the need to care for others as well as yourself.

The fantasy is that your child is all you need. That your life is your child. But reality is showing me that to be a good mom, I also have to develop some other interests.

❧ Check ways you are encouraging healthy independence in your children:

☐ Feed self.   ☐ Put away toys at nap time or bedtime.
☐ Bathe self.   ☐ Straighten bedclothes.
☐ Fold/put away laundry.   ☐ Tie shoes.
☐ Dress self.   ☐ Turn on/off lights.
☐ Brush teeth.   ☐ Comb/brush hair.

☐ List other possibilities: _____

Your World Needs You to Develop Yourself.

All around you are those who need what you have to offer. Whether it is something you do or just a normal outgrowth of the person you are, your contribution to the lives of others is increased when you develop yourself. Seeing you interact with confidence, using innate gifts and learned skills will encourage others to discover ways in which they can improve their own lives and relationships. You may not think it is worth much, but to someone who is watching, your example is valuable.

❧ If your dreaming about growth opportunities leads you toward a money-making venture, consider joining the ranks of mothers who earn money by working at home, either out of necessity and/or a desire to develop their skills. Do you wonder if you are cut out for the challenge? Admittedly, success demands self-discipline and the art of self-starting. Here are some self-examining questions to help you decide:

1. What God-given skills and talents can I channel into a home-based job?

_____

2. Where in my home can I situate my workplace? _____

3. Is there a market for my services? _____

How saturated is the market you want to enter? The local chamber of commerce or a phone book's Yellow Pages can provide clues. Conduct an informal survey of how they are doing. If already established businesses seem to have more customers than they can handle, there probably is room for competition.[1]

God Desires Our Growth.

"Grow in the grace
and knowledge
of our Lord and
Savior Jesus Christ."
2 Peter 3:18

Above all, it is God's plan for us to grow. "God loves us where we are, but he loves us too much to leave us there," reads a popular wall hanging. The Bible directs us to "grow in grace and knowledge" (2 Pet. 3:18). In fact, the goal of the Christian life is to develop such Christlike qualities as love, joy, peace, patience, kindness, and goodness. The mothering season of life offers fertile soil for all of these. Yet growth doesn't occur without a struggle.

Just as we are learning the character traits of a Christian, we need to impart these to our children. In his collection, *The Book of Virtues,* William J. Bennett explains, "The vast majority of Americans share a respect for certain fundamental traits of character: honesty, compassion, courage, and perseverance. These are virtues. But because children are not born with this knowledge, they need to learn what true virtues are."[2]

As followers of Christ, we are responsible to develop all the gifts and abilities God has given us. Read 1 Corinthians 12:27-31. Explain which gifts you contribute to "the body of Christ."

_____

Tell what you are doing to develop one or more of these gifts:

_____

_____

Growing Pains

"I can do everything
through him who
gives me strength."
Philippians 4:13

As exciting and fulfilling as developing our potential might be, it is also painful. Growing hurts. It stretches us in new directions. It uses muscles, both mental and emotional, which may have atrophied from lack of use. It demands risks that may leave us feeling vulnerable and exposed.

Change is often inconvenient and uncomfortable. Suppose you decide you will (finally) accept a position of leadership in your church or your community only to discover that you get very nervous when speaking in front of even small gatherings.

Will you fulfill the commitment ... or quit? If you stick it out, you'll have some stretching to do. You'll have to learn to major on your strengths and delegate to others the areas in which you are lacking. The decision to grow is often accompanied by pain as change occurs. Several realizations may hit you hard.

Growth Is Slow.

It takes time to grow. During the time of life when our young children are growing like weeds, personal growth can seem tortoise-like. Life unfolds in slow motion. Like an instant replay in sports, each event unwinds in torturous tediousness, often replaying through the day. Growth takes time.

Personal growth can seem tortoise-like.

♣ Think of a new skill you learned within the last 3-5 years. How long did it take you to become proficient at it?

(circle)   *a few months*   *1 or more years*   *still learning!*

♣ Reread *This Week's Verse* on page 33. What is God's promise to us, even when growth seems to take a very long time?

_____

Growth Is Hard to Measure.

There are many hectic days when you can hardly tell if you're growing or shrinking. You can stand your three-year-old against the wall and see tangible evidence of his growth by marking a spot two inches above last year's measurement. But when you look at your own life, all you can see growing is the hair on your legs!

The intangibility of the growth of character makes sticking with our goals seem discouraging. Infants don't praise us when we master patience or excel in child care. And when we go to the wall to mark our progress, the results of our efforts may not even be noticeable.

Growth Is Costly.

Whether developing dreams or character, growth costs. If you're working on your piano technique or earning credit toward a college degree, you can expect to make some tough choices. For example, you may choose to read a book during your child's nap time and then serve store-bought deli dinners instead of a homemade meal. Or, if you're wrestling with humility or learning how to be more assertive, you'll have to choose to admit when you're wrong or stand up for yourself when you're right.

Alongside the costly choices is the reality of accepting the consequences for these choices. Your husband may be disappointed with frozen macaroni and cheese for dinner and may communicate his displeasure in no uncertain terms. Or, when you realize you've been wrong in a relationship, you'll have to apologize. Or, if you're struggling with assertiveness, there will be times you're forced to take an uncomfortable stand.

Every achievement has a price tag.

In his book, *The Pursuit of Excellence*, Ted Engstrom writes: "Every truly worthwhile achievement of excellence has a price tag. The question you must answer for yourself is, How much am I willing to pay in hard work, patience, sacrifice and endurance to be a person of excellence?"[3]

Growth—slow, hard to measure, and costly—often brings pain along with its rewards.

♣ Indicate the degree to which you are willing to spend the time and pay the price to continue growing during this stage in your life. Put an X on the seesaw.

not willing   *interested but overwhelmed*   *willing*

Dreaming Dreams

Dream? Ha! Are you joking? Who has the time or energy?

So? Dreams make the difference between living a life and really *living* a life. But some of us, caught up in the busyness of childrearing, have forgotten how to dream. Here are some suggestions:

Dare to Dream.

Identify where you want to grow and then start dreaming about possibilities for getting there. One writer comments, "We must dream, because we are made in the image of him who sees things that are not and wills them to be."[4]

Find a quiet spot. Sit back and let your thoughts roam. What has God already done in your life? What might He still do? Just for a moment, consider what isn't—but could be. Dream beyond where you are.

Dreams begin with asking such questions as, "If you could do anything you wanted with an extra hour today, what would it be?" Sometimes dreams have their roots in the past. "When you think back over your childhood, what did you do with your spare time?" Dreams also peer around the corners of our lives and right into the places we live providing clues as to how we can grow.

As Barbara Sher encourages in her book *Wishcraft*, the important thing is to find what you love. "There may be several things ... whatever they are—guitar music, bridges, bird-watching, sewing, the stock market, the history of India—there is a very, very good reason why you love them. Each one is a clue to something inside you: a talent, an ability, a way of seeing the world that is uniquely yours."[5]

Identify where you want to grow. Then start dreaming a dream for your life and make a plan. A 33-year-old man, recently named to a head coaching position at a major university, deflected questions about being so young for such an important position. "My parents taught me to dream with my feet on the ground. That means I dreamed about where I wanted to go and then made a plan about how to get there."

✿ If you don't have a dream, here are some questions and ideas to help you identify an area of passion and potential in your life:

1. Is there a subject that always sparked your interest?

_____

2. What did you daydream about as a child? _____

3. List 10 of your positive characteristics. _____

_____

_____

Ask a friend to add to the list. Do these traits suggest any talents or skills worth pursuing? If so, which ones?

_____

4. In the margin, list 10 things you want to do before you die. Narrow the list to 5. Then rank in order of importance.

Sequence Your Dreams.

Once you've settled on an area of potential growth, break it down into small sections. We all know that the years of mothering young children are filled with responsibilities and urgent tasks. If we set out to accomplish gargantuan achievements during these years, we'll probably be disappointed, because something will suffer—our children, our marriages, our dreams, or our health.

Have you ever heard someone compare life to a book, with each stage of development occupying its own chapter? During your early life, you eagerly scribbled out your contribution on the clean pages of the first few chapters. But with the

I used to sit in the park with my baby and wonder what had happened to art, music, and politics. I felt isolated from the life I'd known for 20 years, so I decided to do something about it. One day I put my baby in the backpack and went to a show on impressionistic art at the museum.

arrival of children, your own journaling has been put on hold, while you help your child learn to hold his crayon and write in his book of days.

Rather than setting your own journal completely aside for the next few years of childrearing, why not take time to record a few chapters—perhaps a single page or even a whole chapter? We can make progress toward our dreams a little at a time.

This idea of outlining life in chapters—breaking it down into sections—is sometimes called sequencing. In this context, sequencing means giving priority to children when they are young. Then, as they grow older, pursuing our own personal goals, including the development of our dreams.

❀ Select one of your dreams. In the space provided, write what you can do to bring your dream to reality using sequencing:

What I can do while my children are preschoolers _____

_____

What I can do while my children are school-aged _____

_____

What I can do when my children leave the nest _____

_____

Tell Someone Else About Your Dream.

Everyone needs a nudger—someone to champion dreams, someone to encourage him or her to keep dreaming even when the dream seems impossible. Dottie Mc-Dowell, wife of Josh McDowell, describes her mother as a dream-nudger who always valued what Dottie valued: "As an adult, she still dreams my dreams, wanting to know every detail and delighting in every interest that I pursue. Does this communicate that my dreams and goals have significance? You bet it does! Has that had a positive impact on my self-image—even as an adult? Of course."[6]

Everyone needs a nudger—someone to champion dreams.

Maybe you have a good friend who is also dreaming while mothering. Maybe your husband knows the gifts within you and longs with you for them to be developed. Maybe your mother or aunt or sister remembers your dream and will remind you of your personal potential. Seek a nudger who can help keep your dream alive.

❀ A nudger is a person who encourages you to dream and then to act on your dreams. Do you have a nudger in your life?

Write the name of your nudger here. If you don't have one, who might be your

nudger, if asked?_____

Identify some people who have served as nudgers in your past. _____

_____

How did they specifically nudge you?_____

_____

What qualities would you look for in a nudger? _____

_____

List persons for whom you might serve as a nudger. _____

_____

Get Growing

All of us have great, untapped potential. As William James once observed: "Compared with what we ought to be, we are only half awake. Our fires are dampened, our drafts are checked. We are making use of only a small part of our possible mental and physical resources." So nurture your need to grow. We were created by God to grow and change and develop.

I'm a good mother, but I don't want to discover someday that my kids are grown and I have nothing else in my life.

🌸 Reread the *Mothering Maxim* on page 33. Have you set some goals for what you hope to become? List some growth goals in each of the following areas:

Character qualities

_____

_____

_____

Mothering skills

_____

_____

Relationship skills

_____

_____

Be Inspired

"'No eye has seen, no ear has heard, no mind has conceived what God has prepared for those who love him.'"

1 Corinthians 2:9

Louise Driscoll encourages us to hang in there in her poem, "Hold Fast Your Dream."

Hold fast your dream!
Within your heart
Keep one still secret spot
Where dreams may go,
And sheltered so,
May thrive and grow—
Where doubt and fear are not.
Oh, keep a place apart
Within your heart,
For little dreams to go.[7]

As Brenda Hunter writes: "When God gives you a dream, he will help you to realize it. It may take a year or half a lifetime, but God planted that dream in your consciousness for a reason. God and you will make dreams become realities."[8]

Intimacy

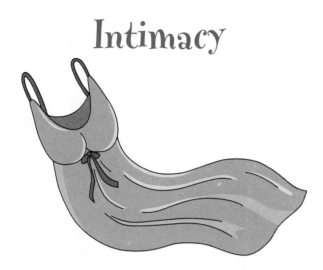

Sometimes I Long to Be Understood

Five-thirty. Dinnertime. Barb opened the refrigerator and surveyed the boring contents. *It's hard to cook for just me and the kids*, she thought. *I hate it when Paul is out of town.* But then, it was more than dinnertime that made Barb miss Paul.

Making a quick decision, she called to Nathan and Kelli: "Hey, kids! We're going for hamburgers!" Whoops and hollers preceded their wild dash for the car. Barb gathered up little Emily in her infant seat, grabbed her purse, and followed.

The parking lot was crowded, so she cautioned Nathan and Kelli to hold hands and walk in front of her. In line, Barb balanced the infant seat and gently guided the other two until they reached the front of the line and ordered.

They all slid into a booth, and Barb began the task of squeezing out catsup, securing crooked lids on drinks, and wiping greasy fingers with napkins.

Nathan and Kelli downed three-quarters of their burgers and fries and begged to go to the play area. Since she could keep an eye on them through the window near the booth, Barb agreed.

Glancing around the crowded room, she saw—in the booth diagonal to hers—a young mom and dad holding hands while smiling at their chubby-faced toddler. One table down was a group of loud teenagers, cocky and oblivious to all around them. Behind her, another mom seemed to be in deep conversation with her preteen daughter. Everyone she saw seemed content and connected to someone.

She looked outside. Nathan and Kelli were playing happily. Emily had dozed off in her infant seat. Barb sighed as she played idly with her straw. With her index

This Week's Verse
"We love because he first loved us."
1 John 4:19

Mothering Maxim
Being understood by another helps me understand myself.

finger, she plugged the top of the straw, then lifted it from her Diet Coke® and let the liquid trickle out. People came and went through the restaurant doors. Meanwhile, Barb felt a familiar longing. Loneliness. It seemed absurd. How could she sit in this room filled with people and feel alone? How could she *ever* feel lonely with three children around her every minute?

Stop! Barb scolded herself. *You have three healthy kids and a husband with a good job. Isn't that enough?* It should be, she reasoned, yet she longed for someone to talk to. Someone who would understand her fears and her struggles with contentment and patience.

Just then, a woman about her age, carrying a tray laden with kid's meals, slid into the booth next to hers. Two little boys—about five and seven years old—followed. From the mother's face, Barb could tell she was a woman who loved what she was doing, even as she patiently squeezed out catsup, straightened crooked lids on drinks, and wiped greasy fingers with napkins.

When her boys ran off to the play area, the woman looked up and her eyes met Barb's. Across the cluttered table, she smiled, "So you're eating gourmet tonight, too?"

Barb laughed and suddenly she felt better. Here they were—total strangers. They would probably never see each other again. But in those few words and for the first time in ages, Barb felt understood.

🌸 If you had been Barb, underline your probable reaction:

I would have invited the woman to my booth for further conversation.

I would have continued to try to talk across the booths.

I would have dropped my eyes and said no more.

That One and Only Lonely Feeling

Keeping up with the kids isn't the hardest part of mothering; it's the loneliness.

Mothers of preschoolers overwhelmingly report that their greatest struggle is with loneliness, a feeling of being disconnected or isolated. Though the words may vary, the feelings describe a common need for intimacy—a longing to be understood.

Ouch! Loneliness hurts. It stings. It sucks out all the filling inside a woman and pierces the exposed, unprotected places.

"God makes a home for the lonely; He leads out the prisoners into prosperity, Only the rebellious dwell in a parched land."
Psalm 68:6

Loneliness hurts so much because it blocks what we intrinsically need as humans. "The Bible proclaims our need for connection," says psychologist John Townsend in his book, *Hiding from Love*. "At the deepest spiritual and emotional level, we are beings who need safety and a sense of belonging in our three primary relationships: God, self, and others. We begin life in a terrified and disconnected state. ... It is the deepest and most fundamental problem we can experience."[1]

In other words, our need for connection is a need created within us by God. He created us to be in relationships with others. And this need or *longing* is answered by a sense of *belonging,* which is also known as being in community. We are said to be in community when we are connected to others in some context of meaningful relationships in which we have a sense of belonging and a shared sense of nurturing and being nurtured.

❀ Do you feel this need for belonging? Place an X on the seesaw to indicate the extent to which loneliness characterizes you at this point in your life?

extremely lonely   *extremely connected*

Loneliness is on the increase. But today's frantic lifestyle simply doesn't lend itself to being in community. Heidi Brennan, who works with a national advocacy group, Mothers at Home, remarks: "People miss the backyard fence. Even working women. Women are community people and even in the workplace, we attempt to create a sense of community."[2]

At-home mothers are critically aware of this need. Author and psychologist Brenda Hunter quotes one mom in her book, *The Company of Women:* "Since I've become a full-time mother, my friends have become very important in creating a new peer group, a sense of community and support as I tackle the difficult task of mothering."[3]

Most of my friends work, so there's no time for friendship, except at night when I'm too tired.

🌿 Whenever you're feeling lonely, take the initiative! Check the activities that you could do:
- ☐ Call someone.
- ☐ Write a letter or note.
- ☐ Turn solitude into quiet time with your best Friend. Read John 15:15 in the margin.
- ☐ Get on the Internet.
- ☐ Make plans with a friend.

"I no longer call you servants, because a servant does not know his master's business. Instead, I have called you friends, for everything that I learned from my Father I have made known to you." John 15:15

We have this need for community—for intimacy—but before we can find it and invest in it, we have to know what it is ... and what it is *not.*

Explaining Intimacy

What is intimacy? The word alone evokes all kinds of images! Isn't intimacy sex? Hugs and kisses and touching? Well ... yes and no. Intimacy may involve sexual expression and physical communication, but intimacy is more than sex.

Well, then, isn't intimacy something like romance? Again, the answer is yes ... and no. Intimacy may be romantic at times. But it doesn't have to be.

OK. Intimacy is like having a constant companion who knows you inside and out and likes you, warts and all. Right? Again, yes and no. The truth is, intimacy rarely occurs in one relationship alone. In fact, when we depend upon only one relationship for our intimacy, we often end up strangling that partnership with too many expectations. Our healthy need for intimacy should not be satisfied in only one place.

The Latin word for *inner* or *innermost* is *intimus*. From this root comes our word *intimate*. Webster defines *intimate* as intrinsic, essential, that which characterizes one's deepest nature, personal.

Another popular definition of the word *intimacy* takes the meaning home to everyday life. Intimacy means "Into-me-see." When we are intimate with someone, we allow him to see into our characters, our personhoods. We become transparent and feel safe to admit our fears and longings.

After I had my first baby I felt that my whole outlook was changing. I was suddenly needed for everything my little baby did. One day everything was going wrong. My son wouldn't have anything to do with me—I—the one who did everything for him. I couldn't get him to eat, stop crying. If I tried to hold him, he screamed and kicked at me. I called my mother, crying uncontrollably, and asked her to please come over and help me, to tell me what I was doing wrong. She managed to calm my son and me, then she just listened and nodded every now and then to everything I felt and said.

> After moving to our fourth home in four years with children ages one and four, the thought of making new friends was too overwhelming, so I just stayed at home with the kids and felt lonely.

What is intimacy? To a mother of preschoolers, the definition is simple. Intimacy is being understood. It's not being judged for what you did wrong this time. It's not being told what you could do differently next time. It's not being corrected, interpreted, or "fixed." Intimacy is being understood, sometimes when you don't even understand yourself.

"It is impossible to overemphasize the immense need people have to be listened to, to be taken seriously, to be understood," writes Paul Tournier. "No one can develop freely in this world and find a full life without feeling understood by at least one person."[4]

❧ Reread the *Mothering Maxim* on page 45. Explain why this statement is true.

Stumbling Blocks to Intimacy

Even when we recognize our needs for intimacy, we find some obstacles that block our pathways to experiencing it.

I'm Too Tired to Be Friendly.

There's no arguing with the reality that moms of preschoolers have very little energy to spend on intimacy. After four nights with little sleep because of a teething, fussy six-month-old, keeping up with the constant responsibility of putting meals on the table, cleaning up, and doing laundry, few of us have energy left over for friends.

Moms are often too tired to relate well even to their husbands.

With the onset of parenthood, I often felt tired and put my husband in last place. I remember one particularly exhausting day when, by the time we got into bed, all I wanted to do was sleep. That's not what he had in mind, but I was too tired to care.

Many parents of preschoolers mourn the lack of time for couple intimacy. In your Bible read 1 Corinthians 7:3-5. What does Paul say is the problem with making a habit of postponing sexual expression?

_____

Which of these would increase the possibilities of couple intimacy at your house? (check all that apply)

☐ Put the kids to bed earlier.
☐ Choose times other than bedtime.
☐ Plan regular get-away weekends.
☐ Schedule sex—that's right, put it on your *personal* calendars.

☐ Other ideas? _____

I Don't Want to Risk Making a Friend Because One of Us Will Just Move Away.

In our mobile society, few of us stay in one place long enough to put down the roots necessary to build intimacy. We're separated from our hometowns and the long-term relationships with people who "knew us when," and we fear that we can never be "known" again.

I Don't Have Time to Be Friendly.

"Women today don't have time for relationships," says Heidi Brennan. "We're more task-oriented in the '90s than earlier, and friendship takes a lot of time."[5] Psychologist Brenda Hunter goes on to comment, "It takes fallow, kickback time to nurture relationships, and with the cultural emphasis on achievement ... friendships with other women are the first to go."[6]

If we're employed and mothering, we let go of friendships in order to survive. If we're mothering without external employment, we often look around the neighborhood, only to find that no one else is available during our few and free precious daytime moments. And when a husband comes home, his needs and the needs of the children come first, ahead of intimacy with friends.

I need someone who understands what I'm saying even when I don't understand it myself.

I need someone to unload on, someone to listen to me.

I'm Uncomfortable with Being Friendly.

Every one of us understands the ongoing struggle to be appropriately intimate. Some of us think it might be easier and maybe even more mature to remain independent of intimate relationships. "No one has trouble understanding why Adam couldn't live alone in paradise," writes Joan Wulff, "but we somehow tell ourselves we can make it alone in today's world."[7]

Others face fear and uncertainty about responsibilities when it comes to developing relationships. As Richard Fowler observes, "Anxiety in interpersonal relationships stems not from a complete unwillingness to socialize or respond, but from confusion about what our roles should be in nurturing and developing relationships."[8]

Perhaps we've been locked into unhealthy relationships in the past and are afraid we'll repeat those old habits. Or maybe we've observed less-than-perfect models of intimacy and so we wonder what exactly is normal and healthy.

"A friend is a present you give yourself."
Robert Louis Stevenson

Some of us defeat ourselves, refraining from embracing the very thing we need. A newspaper article about loneliness explains: "Lonely people are more critical of themselves, more disappointed with others and less willing to take risks in social situations. They are afraid of closeness and actually talk themselves out of being connected to others. They'd rather feel depressed and alone than risk rejection."[9]

✿ When we are depressed, we often interpret excuses as rejection. Check the statements below which you believed to be rejection rather than sincere excuses.

☐ "I've already made plans." ☐ "I have to work."
☐ "I'm not feeling well." ☐ "I have a sick child."
☐ "I have to help my child with homework." ☐ "I'm short on cash right now."

☐ Other? _____

We're too tired; we live in a transient society; we don't have time; we're uncomfortable with intimacy. In her book *No More Lone Ranger Moms*, Donna Partow quotes a woman who sums up the stumbling blocks to intimacy: "My family is several hundred miles away and my husband works from three o'clock in the afternoon to midnight. I hardly ever see him. I was always a loner, but I never felt lonely until I became a mom."[10]

Where to Find Intimacy

Where do we find intimacy? In a variety of places. Intimacy can happen one-on-one with a friend, week after week over coffee. It can occur in marriage when views are exchanged and feelings are respected. Intimacy can happen in a church or group—in community—where feelings are shared.

Rather than taking place only in a single ultra-close relationship, intimacy most likely will transpire in many exchanges over a lifetime and, sometimes, in several spots in one day. In a certain social life, a mom might find intimacy in one particular friendship. Then in other stages, she might find it in another. Intimacy can even happen between total strangers who share a moment of understanding over Happy Meals® at McDonald's.

Before looking at some places to find intimacy, here's a word of caution about where *not* to look for it. Don't look for intimacy with your children. Sure—they're available. They have our attention, and they have our hearts. But it is not their responsibility to meet *our* needs; they should not feel that kind of pressure. "Children do not exist to please us," writes author and professor Walter Wangerin. "They are not for us at all, but rather we exist for them, to protect them now and prepare them for the future."[11]

There may be a time for intimacy with our children when they are adults, but moms who look to their children to meet those needs are looking in the wrong place. When we're looking for intimacy, we should look in places with appropriate potential.

> My husband says he feels like I love our children more than him, and fear grips my heart when I realize that he might be right.

✿ Check the situations below that in your opinion reflect inappropriate intimacy with a child.

- ☐ discussing marriage problems
- ☐ sharing negative feelings about yourself
- ☐ telling your child how much you love him (her)
- ☐ complaining about your husband
- ☐ telling a family secret
- ☐ crying
- ☐ talking about sex
- ☐ fretting about finances

Marriage

Our relationships with our life partners are the most likely, and certainly the most important, sources of intimacy. They are also the most challenging. Added to the stress of caring for children is the sense that an escalating divorce rate in our society makes marriage a less-than-safe place.

Why is intimacy in marriage such a struggle? Besides the obvious stumbling blocks to intimacy—fatigue, transience, lack of time, unhealthy relational patterns—there are several hurdles to overcome as we establish intimacy in marriage.

For example, men and women may interpret intimacy differently. When one partner seeks intimacy, he may be looking for companionship or sex. For the other, intimacy may mean the close connection of being understood.

In addition, babies—whether one or many—change the marriage relationship. In some ways the change is wonderful, as author Dale Hanson Bourke tells a friend contemplating motherhood: "My friend's relationship with her husband will change, but not in the way she thinks. I wish she could understand how much

> I need to be able to talk to my husband about the things that are nearest and dearest to my heart, but it is hard for me to be vulnerable and step out in faith and trust him with my emotions.

Even when my baby was asleep, I had no time for my husband because one ear was always tuned to listen for her cry. I couldn't stop thinking about the baby.

more you can love a man who is always careful to powder the baby or who never hesitates to play with his son or daughter. I think she should know that she will fall in love with her husband again for reasons she would now find very unromantic."[12]

There's another response, however. It's the "down" side of the up-and-downness of adjusting to a new baby. Slowly a husband and wife realize that their communication patterns have changed. They are less intimate, more custodial.

Motherhood introduces a different wrinkle in a wife's relationship with her husband. Many moms admitted falling in love with their new babies, the kind of surprising, consuming love that sometimes closed out their husbands. In the margin read observations from three moms who commented on the changes parenthood brought to their marriages.

My husband and I keep learning so much about ourselves and each other through parenthood. And we keep having to face new fears and make changes in ourselves that impact our relationship.

❀ Answer these questions about the level of intimacy in your marriage by circling T for true or F for false:

T F   I maintain an active interest in my husband's work and make an effort to keep up with the names, problems, and office politics he shares with me.

T F   My husband and I have made our marriage a priority above our relationship with our children.

T F   We spend time alone each week focusing on our relationship.

T F   My husband and I openly discuss our feelings about house rules for the children, spending, housework, standards, and values.

❀ Overcoming stumbling blocks to intimacy is challenging but rewarding. As you read each suggestion for establishing intimacy with your husband, rate yourself on a scale from 1-5 where 1 = inconsistent and 5 = very consistent.

The day our baby arrived, we suddenly seemed to find an accumulation of differences we had no idea existed. We have to keep reminding ourselves that we are on the same team; we're in this together.

___*Ask.* Ask your husband questions. Just a few at a time. Probing, curious questions. Interesting questions. Questions that encourage him to be open, to share his dreams. What is his greatest dream in life? If he could do anything he chose with his time when he turns 50, what would it be? What three adjectives would he like others to use in describing him?

___*Listen.* After asking, listen. Open your ears and take in all you hear. Resist the urge to critique, redirect, evaluate. Just listen, accepting whatever you hear as having worth and value because it reflects something about the one you love.

___*Act.* After asking and listening, act on what you heard. Did you catch that tone in his voice—the one that says he's afraid you won't take him seriously? Did you grab that chance to compliment him in front of your friends? Lock eyes and wink from across a room. Share a private joke. Squeeze his hand in church.

___*Risk.* It's not enough to receive the shared soul of another person. If we want to establish true intimacy with another, we must take the risk to unveil who we are as well.

___*Adjust.* Marriages change. And they should, because the people involved change. As we invest in intimacy, we must be open to adjusting ourselves within our relationships.

___*Forgive.* "Opposites attract—until they get married" is a familiar saying. So we have to practice the art of forgiving—and the art of not holding grudges. A pastor advised a soon-to-be-married couple to "keep short accounts" and then quoted Scripture: "Do not let the sun go down while you are still angry" (Eph. 4:26). The habit of holding onto grudges becomes a brick wall to building and nurturing intimacy.

Ask. Listen. Act. Risk. Adjust. Forgive. All of these are suggestions for building intimacy with spouses. In general, the ongoing kindling of intimacy in a marriage takes time, effort, and intentionality, but the effort will strengthen and protect your relationship with your mate.

But remember, seeking intimacy in marriage alone puts too much strain on the relationship. As Cecil Osborne says in his book, *The Art of Understanding Your Mate,* "There are no perfect marriages for the simple reason there are no perfect people, and no one person can satisfy all of one's needs."[13]

Don't expect your husband to meet all your needs. He can't. Moms of preschoolers, whether married, single, or separated geographically from family and friends, need the intimacy of friendships. Writer and mother Valerie Bell described this revelation recently to some MOPS members:

As a young wife and mother, I remember sitting by our front bay window, playing the "counting game" with my two small sons. It went like this: "How long do you think it will be 'til Daddy comes home? I bet if we count to 50, he'll be here." Daddy rarely came on the first count. For the boys, it was a game. For me—a young mom isolated with their care all day long—the number counting was not a game. Every lonely number was filled with a longing for my husband who happened to be my major link to the outside world.

Then one morning, a woman about my age showed up on my doorstep with doughnuts and her two children. Her name was Rosie.

"Let's have breakfast, let's talk, let's be friends." She was a lifeline that morning and uncountable other mornings as we shared our secrets, took comfort in the mutual naughtiness of our children, laughed and dreamed and cried and prayed together. Her friendship gave me a link to the outside world and a unique kind of connection that even my husband couldn't provide.

I have a need to find my kindred spirit, my bosom buddy. Someone who is just like me. Someone who likes to do activities with the kids and would be loving and accepting of who I am.

Friendships

After marrying and having children, I lost touch with all female friends and devoted myself fully to my family. I miss the one-on-one talks and camaraderie of female friends.

One after another, moms cry out for the understanding provided uniquely through women friends. This need started early in life. Most females remember their "first best friend" during preadolescence, a friend with whom to share secrets, write notes, and have weekend sleepovers. During teenage years, best friends start competing with boyfriends, a competition that often lasts during courtship and the first few years of marriage. But then another stage begins, when many husbands are working hard and many moms with young children greatly need close women friends again.

❧ Often we look for friends exactly like us when there is much to be gained from establishing a friendship with someone from a different culture, background, racial group, or generation. Such a situation might present certain challenges—stretching or adjusting our attitudes—but these special friendships can enlarge and encourage as well. Check places you could meet these types of friends:

☐ community college   ☐ nursing homes
☐ gyms/exercise classes   ☐ mission/ethnic churches
☐ city parks/recreation facilities ☐ community centers

I have many friends and I cherish each one. But I pray to meet a friend who can be my best friend. Her husband and my husband click, our children get along. We spend time together baking, having tea, laughing together ...

Even in friendships we must overcome some unique stumbling blocks. For example, we might be tempted to idealize a friend as the cure-all for our problems during these days of raising needy young ones, or we may long for the perfect friend who doesn't exist. But just as no marriage can meet our every need for intimacy, neither can a single friendship or wished-for best friend. We must be realistic.

Another barrier to friendship is being overly possessive. At times, we act like a two-year-old who must first claim an object as "Mine!" before it can be shared with others, or a five-year-old who demands that a friend be her best and *only* friend. In friendship, as in marriage, possessiveness suffocates. But, unlike marriage, the mark of the most mature friendship may be the open-handedness of sharing our friends with other friends.

We also must recognize that friends come and go during different seasons or arenas of life. Friends move away. Circumstances change. For example, a once intimate friend in the workplace may have less in common now that you're a mom. One woman recently differentiated between "friends for the road" and "friends for the heart." Not every friend is meant to be our best friend, and not every relationship is meant to be forever. "'Friends for the road' are the people God puts in our life for a short time or a specific purpose. But a friend for the heart ... that's the friendship that's meant to last."[14]

❀ Remember this oldie but goodie? "You've got to be a friend to have a friend." Underline below ways you can be a friend to others. Double underline those tactics you have practiced.

A good friend overlooks your broken-down gate and admires the flowers in your window.
Anonymous

don't talk about yourself all the time.

keep a confidence.

listen more than you talk.

be honest but tactful.

open up to others; often they'll do the same.

listen non-judgmentally.

be willing to try new activities/adventures.

stay away from gossip.

be available when your friend needs you.

be willing to initiate contact.

One other piece of advice about close friends: when we transfer a relationship of emotional intimacy from a husband to a friend, we border on the problem of committing *emotional* adultery. For the married woman, friendships are meant to complement and complete the need for intimacy, not replace it so that emotional intimacy is unnecessary or neglected in the marriage relationship.

Once we understand the possible barriers to intimacy in friendship, how can we begin establishing close relationships? Identify what you value most in a friendship, then work on developing and modeling those qualities in yourself. Perhaps you prefer a companion who will listen without interrupting or judging. Then close your mouth and open your ears when you listen. You may want an outdoorsy type who enjoys fresh air and exercise. So get out there and start walking. Maybe you'll meet your friend along the hiking trail!

Seek Friends on "Common Ground."

During this season of life, moms need other moms to share their joys and struggles. Seek friends with common circumstances, such as other mothers of young children or other moms with "special needs" children. Look for support groups that meet your unique needs.

MOPS, designed for mothers of preschoolers, meets in churches all around the country. Call the MOPS Headquarters (800-929-1287) or check the Web site at http://www. MOPS.org to find a group in your area.

❀ It's time to develop an action plan. Read the following list of opportunities to make and nurture friendships. Then go back and rank them from 1-8 in the order you plan to pursue them. Get going on the one you ranked first.

___*Volunteer.* The more you do in your community, the greater your chances for meeting people. Sharing work promotes good conversation and mutual respect.

___*Combine activities.* Integrate your daily errands or exercise routines with friends. For example, arrange for your and your friend's children to take ballet or swim lessons at the same time.

___*Be a special events organizer.* Scan the entertainment section for details about special events of interest to mothers and their children and invite a group to participate. Call two or three mothers and ask them to meet you for a picnic in the park.

___*If a friendship is in trouble, analyze the cause.* Apologize if you have hurt someone. If your friend has hurt you, let her know how you feel as clearly and lovingly as you can. Remember that part of friendship is forgiving shortcomings.

___*Don't be afraid to request favors.* In creating obligations to one another as friends we bond more deeply. Be careful to return favors and borrowed goods in good shape and within reasonable amounts of time.

___*Stay in touch.* Can you remain friends with your working friends? Of course. As long as you keep up other interests besides your baby's most recent diaper rash or a new baby product, you'll find plenty to talk about.

___*Don't let treasured friends drift away.* Make a standing monthly date for lunch or dinner. Scheduling it on the calendar ups the chances of it actually happening.

___*Be spontaneous.* On the spur of the moment, call a new friend to just chat and remind her that you care.

Let Jesus Be Your Friend

"The world is passing away, and also its lusts; but the one who does the will of God abides forever."
1 John 2:17

When you grow old and look back at these mothering years, we hope you will be able to say that the truest Friend, the most dependable Friend, the One who loved you most is Jesus. Someday all earthly friendships and relationships will come to an end, but a relationship with Jesus continues on into eternity. Doesn't it make sense to develop that intimate relationship with Him now?

🍀 How are you seeking to grow in your friendship with Jesus? (circle all that apply)

daily Bible reading	*daily prayer*	*Bible study with a group*
service through my church	*sharing my faith*	*obedience to His Word*

🍀 Reread *This Week's Verse* on page 45. Today think about the words to a familiar children's song: "Jesus loves me, this I know. For the Bible tells me so." Insert your name in place of the word *me.*

Week 5

Instruction

Sometimes I Don't Know What to Do

This Week's Verse
"Teach me your way, O Lord, and I will walk in your truth." Psalm 86:11

Mothering Maxim
An informed mother knows best.

Three-year-old Benjamin screeched loudly, "No! I don't want to sit at the table, and you can't make me!" Ruthie shot her husband David a look of panic across the table. Benjamin was about to throw a tantrum right here in front of her in-laws and all of David's brothers and sisters and their perfectly behaved children. And she didn't have a clue as to what to do about it.

"He's tired." She smiled weakly, searching for some excuse for her child's poor behavior. "After all, we've been riding in the car for nearly eight hours."

At that moment, David grabbed Benjamin and tried to force him into his seat at the table. Ruthie could see the tension in her husband's face.

"Daddy! Let go of my arm! I want Mommy!" Benjamin wailed.

Ruthie reached out for him, but he swung away and ran screaming toward the kitchen. Both Ruthie and David dashed after him while all the relatives watched. Without even looking, Ruthie could sense the judgment on their faces.

"Ruthie!" David exclaimed as he caught the child. "I told you we shouldn't have given him that Coke® at the gas station. Now he's wired, and he'll never settle down!"

Ruthie's forced smile was in place. But beneath the plastic mask, she was churning—against David, against Benjamin, against marriage and three-year-olds and visits to in-laws and decisions like whether or not to give toddlers a Coke® or a spanking or a "time out" ... or what.

How was she supposed to know, anyway? She'd never been a mom before, and her own family had done things so differently. Not that she really wanted to model herself after them, either—at least, not exactly.

I was given the position of mothering without a training manual. I went from the corporate world to being a full-time mom and needed help making the transition. In the working world, I felt confident and in control, but motherhood opened up a world of uncertainty where I realized I had much to learn.

Suddenly, she was very tired of all these questions with no clear answers. Life used to be so much simpler before she became a mother. So many times now she just didn't know what to do!

♣ None of us has all the answers, but we can ask the questions! List some situations or topics you wish you had the answers to when it comes to being a parent.

_____

_____

What's a Mother to Do?

When a woman becomes a mother, she enters foreign territory. We may have observed our own mothers mothering, our grandmothers mothering, a good friend mothering, or even a woman in front of us in line at the grocery store mothering. But we come into mothering ignorant of what it means to mother our own children. Not only that, but during the earliest stages of mothering, we also lack information on how to manage our time while so many other lives are dependent upon ours, how to stay on top of our finances, and how to understand our values and identities as women and mothers.

When we become mothers, we ask the perennial question of motherhood: What's a mother to do?

Questions, Questions, Questions

During pregnancy, I spent a great deal of time preparing for the birth of our child and no time preparing for after the birth. I figured it would come naturally. What a joke!

Mothers express their needs in emotional blurbs. Some questions address the basics of how to get through the day, or how to diaper the baby, or what to feed him and when.

As we continue mothering, we move past some of the survival skill questions only to face other questions that focus more on complex skills. A survey of moms in a woman's magazine revealed that their confidence declined as their children aged and their mothering focus deepened to substantive issues. Beyond simply surviving, how do we nurture the lives of those who have been entrusted to us? The questions are endless.

♣ Read the following list of questions. Star the ones you've successfully worked your way through. Underline issues that still pose problems.

How do I handle my mother-in-law's judgment of how I'm mothering?
How should I discipline? Should I spank or not? If so, how and until what age?
When should I try potty-training and how in the world do I do it?
What about sibling rivalry? The kids are driving me nuts with their fighting!

How much TV should I let them watch?

What about schooling? Should we go public, private, or home school?

Should I stay home with the kids or work outside the home?

How should I handle money issues?

Whether focused on basic survival skills or on the more complex issues of growth and development, moms of young children are always asking questions. Where will we find the answers we seek?

❋ Think of a decision you are currently facing. Follow these steps in making a wise decision. Then in the margin, record and date your decision.

1. *Pinpoint the problem.* State specifically what it is you need to decide.
2. *Set a deadline.* Give yourself a "due date" for your decision. Develop a time line.
3. *Gather information.* What are your sources? Where can you get the facts?
4. *List the pros and cons.* What are the positives and negatives of each alternative?
5. *Ask tough questions.* Does this fit? Is it wise? Does it conflict with biblical truth?
6. *Make a decision.* Move forward with confidence that you've made the best decision with the available information.

Libraries of Learning

Most moms find that they need to spend time in five libraries of learning during their mothering years: maternal instincts, maternal knowledge, heart values, expert advice, and mothering mentors.

Maternal Instinct

Every mom has a built-in sense of what her child needs. Pediatrician Dr. William Sears observes, "God would not have given you this child without also giving you the means to care for this child."[1] Adoptive mothers cite an innate response that seemed to emerge from within them as their new babies were placed in their arms.

Tough to prove and easy to dismiss, the library of maternal instinct is a place where a mom must learn to trust her heart response to her child.

There's a way in which mothering is instinctive. A mom intrinsically knows her child. The library of maternal instinct teaches moms to trust this instinctive response. Few of us have to be taught to cuddle a baby who is upset. Most of us respond immediately to her cry and can quickly interpret its meaning. Sometimes we wake in the night before he even starts to whimper. Having taken no courses on cooing, babbling, or giggling with our infants, we naturally respond when they speak in this "language."

What do I do when my five-year-old lies {again}? Are my children going to grow up to be productive adults? Are they going to share my belief in God and the values I believe are right? Where does my husband fit in? Am I reading the right books?

I thought my patience level would be much lower. I guess I sold myself short on having what it takes to be a good mother.

❀ Give an example of some aspect of mothering that seemed to come naturally to you:

_____

Maternal Knowledge

When I became pregnant, I took it for granted that mothering would come naturally. The day my baby was born, it hit me like a ton of bricks that mothering did not come naturally to me, and I felt nervous just holding her. I felt totally inadequate as a mother and needed help.

While some aspects of mothering are instinctive, information about what to do and when to do it can be learned. Mothering is a skill that will become easier with knowledge and practice. But some mothers still aren't sure.

The importance of knowing what to do when must not be minimized. We have to learn what medicines help which illnesses, what foods stop diarrhea, when to expect him to crawl and then walk, and how to childproof a home.

Herein lies the great balancing act between heart (maternal instinct) and head (maternal knowledge). Maternal instinct may tell you that your child is not feeling well. Do his eyes look funny? Is he more clingy than normal? Do you sense that something is wrong even though there's no fever? If so, then maternal knowledge will tell you what to do. Take his temperature. Give Tylenol®. Push fluids.

In the library of maternal instinct, we learn to listen with our heart to respond to our child. In the library of maternal knowledge, we learn to find answers. Maternal instinct is innate. Maternal knowledge is acquired. We must have both; they function in tandem.

❀ Explain how this week's *Mothering Maxim* illustrates the balance between knowledge and instinct.

_____

Actions based on instinct alone may lead to overprotection, overreaction, or just plain error. For example, our instinct is to protect our children, but overprotection can paralyze them emotionally. On the other hand, actions based on knowledge alone may overlook subtle truths and harm a sensitive spirit. Seek a balance.

There are times I feel uncertain about what to do. But by talking with other parents and listening to my heart, we manage pretty well.

❀ What is the best way for you to learn new information? Take the inventory of learning styles on pages 67-68 to determine whether you learn best through hearing (auditory), seeing (visual), or touching, doing, or moving (kinesthetic).

Heart Values

Every mom holds to certain core values that she longs to pass on to her children. These values help us make decisions. They inspire us to continue when we'd rather quit. They motivate us to change when we'd rather stay the same. They are our rules for living.

In the library of heart values, we intentionally decide which of these ideals will be communicated and modeled in everyday life—before children, before families, before the world in which we live. Some of us have operated out of a system of rules that has been in place since we were tiny tots ourselves. Others are building on a small base, enlarging as we grow. And still others are just beginning to come to grips with what really matters and are giving it voice, perhaps for the first time.

What do you want your life to stand for? What passions do you want your children to inherit from you? These principles are your mothering maxims. They are guidelines by which to mother. Truths that direct. Absolutes that we want to see our children adopt as their own.

Need some examples? Here's one: "The goal of mothering is to teach a child not to lean on you forever. Mothering is to make leaning unnecessary." At the root of this maxim is the belief that a mother's role in the life of her child is to teach him or her to be an independent individual who can live confidently and competently.

Another? "The Bible is believable today and its principles are applicable to everyday life because the Bible is God's Word." At the core of this maxim is the belief that what the Bible teaches is timelessly true and can be trusted to help us deal with today's challenges. God speaks to us through the Bible.

🍀 Reread *This Week's Verse*, Psalm 86:11, on page 57. Does this verse represent the desire of your heart? ☐ Yes ☐ No
In your Bible, read Deuteronomy 6:6-7. What are some ways you are seeking to teach God's truth?

_____

What are *your* mothering maxims? Knowing what to do in the life of your child, in your marriage, and in your life begins with knowing what is really important to you. Before you look outside yourself for help, look *inside* to see what you value and why.

🍀 Develop your own Mothering Maxims. Maxims are the memorable sayings or statements that shape your attitudes and actions. They sum up your values. Write some of your own. To get you started, here are some questions from Cindy Tolliver's book *At-Home Motherhood*:
  • Think back to your own childhood. Determine some specific things your own mother did that truly made a difference in your life.

_____

What surprised me was the realization that I knew so little about raising a child. I'm not talking about what to dress him in or how to feed him but how to cultivate his unique qualities. The awesomeness of this responsibility has only grown larger in the 21 months since his birth.

- What things did your mother do that you would like to do differently?

  _____

- Think about some mothers you consider to be notable. What do these women do that you might want to include in your mothering mission?

  _____

- In the margin list at least ten goals of mothering using the following guidelines:
  —Let your ideas flow. In brainstorming, there are no right or wrong answers.
  —Make your statements "I-oriented" and active. In other words, don't make your mission dependent on others doing something for you.
  —Make your statements concrete. Instead of saying, "I want to start having fun with my kids," say, "I want to plan at least one fun activity a week with the kids."
  —Pick the five goals that are the most important to you. This doesn't mean you aren't going to accomplish the others, but if you have too many goals, your attention will be spread too thin.[2]

Goal No. 1: _____

Goal No. 2: _____

Goal No. 3: _____

Goal No. 4: _____

Goal No. 5: _____

Expert Advice

I always thought that motherhood would be easy as long as you went by the book, but it didn't take long for me to realize that there is more than one book, and they all say something different.

There are answers, answers, and more answers available to the mother with questions. A myriad of sources compose the library of expert advice. At times, the answers bombard us even before we formulate the questions. Most moms today spend time wandering through the "rows" of available resources.

Take the media, for example. In a season when it's very difficult to get out of the house to seek other input, moms of small children are tempted to hold sacred the views of talk shows, soap operas, radio gurus, and women's magazines. While such sources entertain and inform in part, we must ask whether they offer complete and adequate information. Can we trust them?

There is also the medical profession. Many moms rely on helpful advice from their pediatricians or family practitioners. Questions about everything from earaches to diarrhea find solutions on the medical hotline. A must for any mom.

And then there are the books. Volumes of information are available on every subject under the sun. All this expert advice can be a bit overwhelming.

Moms need some kind of system in order to glean the best from this library of help. Without library tools, we get lost in the card catalog, unsure of where to turn next.

♣ Take a personal field trip to your local library. Don't be intimidated by the computerized listing of books. Someone is always happy to help you. Take advantage of this valuable resource. Report on your outing at your next group session.

I graduated from college with honors, but when I had my first baby, I felt so unsure of what to do. I immediately enrolled in parenting classes at the local hospital and read everything I could.

Several guidelines are helpful as we make our way through the maze of expert opinions.
- *Check credentials.* Every expert comes with a background orientation. Before you adopt his or her advice, read the fine print. Where was the author educated? What are her basic assumptions? Do his values agree with your value base, or do they contradict it?
- *Get a second opinion.* Avoid the temptation to become a follower of only one theory. Wisdom often comes from a multiplicity of sources. Gathering more information helps you make good choices. Research many approaches before you settle on one. And then, throughout your child's development, continue your research and reconsider approaches as her needs change.
- *Be discerning.* Use critical thinking. Ask yourself: Does this approach make sense? Does it contradict my values or common knowledge? Is it consistent with what the Bible teaches?
- *Put advice to a test.* Once you discover advice you think might work, try it out. If it doesn't, adapt it to suit your child's needs. If it still doesn't work, throw it out and go on to another idea.

I heard a speaker on sibling rivalry and then gleaned hints from discussing what was said with others who attended. My kids still fight, but I'm armed with some sound new ideas to help along the way!

One principle from a parenting expert may be appropriate, whereas another may not fit at all. For example, a suggested method of time management may be helpful in the early years of mothering and then become useless as your children age. Before integrating advice into your life and the life of your family, try it out.

The library of expert opinion is one of the most well-stocked sources of instruction available to the mother of preschoolers. Before you begin randomly choosing resources off the shelf, devise a system of discernment that works for you.

♣ In the margin list one or more books you would recommend to others in your study group. If possible, bring it (them) with you to your next group session. Establish a lending library with your friends. Trade tapes, books, and magazines.

Mothering Mentors

Mentoring can offer moms instruction on how to manage time, relationships, and mothering from an up-close-and-personal perspective. Traditionally, a woman's mother assumed this role and instructed her daughter in how to care for an infant and other family-related issues. Unfortunately, many women today don't live near their mothers or share that kind of relationship with their mothers, so the role of mentoring is assumed by others.

In the Greek legend, *The Odyssey*, Mentor was the faithful friend to Ulysses. When Ulysses went to fight in the Trojan War, the care and education of his son, Telemachus, was entrusted to Mentor. In time, the term *mentor* has become a synonym for a wise person, a trusted advisor, a counselor, or teacher.

A mothering mentor is a woman who has scaled the mountain you intend to climb. She knows the path. She knows the toeholds. She comes alongside you and offers encouragement that you, too, can make it. From her life experience, she can teach on such subjects as how to mother, how to organize life, how to develop your abilities and character, or how to hurdle difficult spots in friendship. For a young mother who has never observed good mothering, she might fill the need for a role model. She might also provide a glimpse of what marriage looks like down the road.

A mothering mentor is not a know-it-all. She's not an expert whose name is trailed by degrees and credentials, although she may possess formal training. She is simply a mom who's survived some of the most challenging years of mothering. She's learned from her mistakes, enjoyed a few successes, and can now share her insights with those of us who are only now beginning the journey.

In the local MOPS group, mentors are modeled according to the "Titus woman" principle found in Titus 2:3-4: "Teach the older women to be reverent in the way they live ... to teach what is good. Then they can train the younger women to love their husbands and children, to be self-controlled and pure, to be busy at home, to be kind, and to be subject to their husbands, so that no one will malign the word of God." Ideally, each group benefits from a mentoring mom who shares gently and practically from her life experiences in a group setting and is then available to share one-on-one advice.

Mentors are all around us. They are found in churches, families, and cross-generational friendships. Look for qualities like honesty, wisdom, discernment, and encouragement. Watch from a distance before pursuing a relationship. Then, find the courage to ask if you can poke around a bit to see how she does what she does with her kids. Mentoring doesn't have to be a formal arrangement, nor will you always learn everything you need to know from one single person. Proverbs 10:13 reminds us that "wisdom is found in those who take advice."

❀ Here are some tips on seeking a mentor. Use the margin as a worksheet:

- Determine your mentoring needs. Do you need a coach, an encourager, a counselor, or someone to listen to your ideas? Do you want to sharpen your leader or parenting skills or add spiritual depth? Your needs and goals will determine what kind of mentor is best for you.

- Who are the resourceful women you already know and respect? An aunt or close relative? A godly woman? An older neighbor or friend? Sometimes you can be mentored by a woman younger than yourself if she has unusual qualities or expertise.

- Look for women who are living your dream or share in your dream. Share your desires and objectives with potential mentors. Many older women will be flattered that you consider them worthy of your consideration. Remember, they have a need for generativity—impacting the succeeding generation.

- Be willing to pay the price for mentoring. This includes flexibility and commitment. If she jogs, jog with her. Offer to help with a project so you can learn as you work. Prepare for your time together with specific needs and questions. Your initiative and intentionality will speed and enhance the mentoring process.[3]

❀ Some groups and churches offer formal mentoring relationships through their women's ministry. If you feel God's nudging to be a part of such a program, contact your pastor, women's ministry leader, or other church leader to share your interest. Look for mentoring resources at your LifeWay Christian Bookstore or other Christian bookstore in your area.

Peers

Probably the most common resource for moms is a result of relationships with other moms.

A woman asks a coworker working in the next cubicle what she should do with her unruly toddler. Neighbors swap theories while their preschoolers race around on their tricycles. Though many mothers are separated physically or emotionally from the extended families that could help, some live close enough to relatives to rely on their input.

Many moms are involved in churches where support and instruction come hand-in-hand. Mother's Day Out programs, support groups, or cross-generational relationships offer instruction needed in topics ranging from discipline to budgeting.

I recently was struggling with the amount of time my children were spending watching television. I recalled another mom who had once described her solution to this problem—issuing tickets to watch each TV program. Within three weeks, my children were "weaned" to a minimal amount of TV every day!

🍀 Check a recent church newsletter or bulletin to learn what groups are being offered or planned that would include parenting concerns. Offer to lead a group if none is available. Here are some resources you might want to check out:

Shaping the Next Generation (ISBN 0-7673-3476-0)

Empowered Parenting (ISBN 0-8054-9815-X)

Parenting by Grace (ISBN 0-8054-9939-3)

Breaking the Cycle of Hurtful Family Relationships (ISBN 0-8054-9981-4)

New Faces in the Frame: A Guide to Marriage and Parenting in the Blended Family (ISBN 0-8054-9817-6)

To order, call 1-800-458-2772 or visit your nearest LifeWay Christian Store.

Whether formal or spontaneous, in groups or one-on-one, moms need the supportive community of their peers. After being up all night with a crying baby, a mom finds comfort in chatting on the phone with a friend who also got no sleep. Ah, the support! the camaraderie! the comfort! the answers!

Check out a church nearby for a MOPS group. There you'll find a ready-made audience of women with similar interests. Head to the park on a sunny day or take a walk in your neighborhood and you'll probably locate other moms whose kids are the same age as yours. The library of peers offers the practical advice all moms need.

A Mother's Mission

While children come into the world without an instruction manual, many libraries of learning are available to the moms of young children. Susan Lenzkes' simple poem illustrates our desire to mother the right way while directing us to relax in a trusting posture. Read it in the margin.

A mother's mission includes more than teaching manners and personal hygiene. It is more than homemaking skills or surviving in the work-a-day world. Above all her mission is to train her children in knowing and doing the will of God. God will "equip you with everything good for doing his will" (Heb. 13:21). He has called you to parenting. He equips those He calls!

🖋 Read 2 Timothy 1:5 in your Bible. Paul noted Timothy's "sincere faith." Paul said this faith came from what source?

_____

We model faith day-by-day through our words, attitudes, and actions. Ask God to help you be a consistent model of dependency on Him.

I searched—but there definitely was not a packet of instructions attached to my children when they arrived. And none has since landed in my mailbox. Lord, show me how to be a good parent. Teach me to correct without crushing, help without hanging on, listen without laughing, surround without smothering, and love without limit—the way You love me.[4] *Used by permission, copyright Susan L. Lenzkes, 1981. Available through author.*

Learning Style Inventory

Everyone has a unique style by which they learn best. The following statements can help determine your own unique style. Read each statement, then circle the letter beside your likely response. Answer in the way you might react the majority of the time.

1. You will usually remember more from a lecture when:
   a. you do not take notes but listen very closely;
   b. you sit near the front of the room and watch the speaker;
   c. you take notes (whether or not you look at them again).

2. You usually solve problems by:
   a. talking to yourself or a friend;
   b. using an organized, systematic approach with lists, schedules, and so on;
   c. walking, pacing, or other physical activities.

3. You remember phone numbers when you can't write them down by:
   a. repeating the number to yourself;
   b. "seeing" or "visualizing" the number in your mind;
   c. sketching out the number with your finger on a table or wall.

4. You have to learn something new and it would be easier if you could:
   a. be told how to do it;
   b. watch a demonstration of how to do it;
   c. try it yourself.

5. You remember most from a movie by:
   a. what the characters said, the background noises and music;
   b. the setting, scenery, and costumes or uniforms;
   c. the feelings you had.

6. You go to the grocery store and you:
   a. silently or orally repeat the list to yourself;
   b. walk up and down the aisles to see what you need;
   c. usually remember what you need from your forgotten list at home.

7. You are trying to remember something so you:
   a. replay in your head what was said or any noises that occurred;
   b. try to see it happen in your mind;
   c. feel the way it reacted with your emotions.

8. You learn a foreign language best by:
   a. listening to record or tapes;
   b. using workbooks and writing;
   c. attending a typical class where you read and write.

9. You are confused about the spelling of a word so you:
   a. sound it out;
   b. try to see it written in your mind;
   c. try writing it several ways and choosing the one that looks right.

10. You enjoy reading most when you can read:
    a. dialogue between characters;
    b. descriptive passages that allow you to create mental pictures;
    c. stories with immediate action in the book because it's hard for you to sit still.

11. You usually remember people you have met by their:
    a. names (you forget faces);
    b. faces (you forget names);
    c. walk, mannerisms, motions.

12. You are mostly distracted by:
    a. noises;
    b. people;
    c. environment (temperature, comfort of furniture, and so forth).

13. You usually dress:
    a. fairly well, but clothes are not so important to you;
    b. in a particular style and neatly;
    c. comfortably so you can move around.

14. You can't do anything physical or read, so you choose to:
    a. talk with a friend;
    b. watch TV or look out the window;
    c. move slightly in your chair or bed.

Scoring: In the blanks below, write the total number of responses for each letter.
a. Auditory (learn best by hearing) _____
b. Visual (learn best by seeing) _____
c. Kinesthetic (learn best by touching, doing, moving)[5] _____

Week 6

Help

Sometimes I Need to Share the Load

"What time are the Jacksons coming over tonight?" Randy called to Susan from his comfy chair in front of the TV, the remote control poised in his hand.

Randy had just arrived home from work and looked beat. Susan knew her husband liked to relax on Friday nights, but she was looking forward to having the Jacksons over. Their kids were about the same ages and played well together, which gave the adults a chance to talk without the normal interruptions.

Six o'clock," she called back as she rushed to put some bowls in the dishwasher. "In about ten minutes."

Susan quickly took stock of her dinner preparations. The table was set and the meal basically ready, but Legos® still littered the family room floor. A few stray Play-doh® crumbs crunched under her feet as she shoved the casserole into the oven. Just then the children ran screeching from the bathroom to their bedrooms down the hall.

The bathroom. Ugh! She hadn't cleaned the bathroom yet. Throwing the hot pads on the counter, she took long strides down the hall to the bathroom and flipped on the light. What a mess! Toilet paper hung from everywhere two-feet-high hands could reach. The rest of the roll of paper floated in the toilet. She heard giggles from behind the closed bedroom door down the hall.

Then the doorbell rang.

"Su-u-uszzz! They're here!" Randy yelled.

Stifling a scream, Susan fished out the wet roll of paper and threw it in the wastebasket. She reached for the only towel that matched the bathroom, but it was

This Week's Verse
"God is our refuge and strength, an ever-present help in trouble."
Psalm 46:1

Mothering Maxim
Many hands make little work.

missing. Then she spotted it—a wet wad hiding behind the toilet.

The doorbell rang again. The kids burst from their rooms and ran down the hall toward the front door, giggling and banging against the walls.

"Su-u-uszzz! They're here! Aren't you going to get the door?" Randy called again.

A high-pitched wail emerged from the bathroom. Forming words, the voice screeched: "Hey—am I the *only* one who can answer the door? Am I the *only* one who can make dinner and clean up and watch the kids?" As Susan scooped up the towel from behind the toilet, she realized that the voice was hers. "HEY—DOES ANYONE OUT THERE REALIZE I COULD USE SOME HELP?! I SAID, HELP!!!!!"

The Toughest Question

When mothers of preschoolers were asked, "What do you need most?" they offered a smattering of answers. In the margin, read some of their replies:

A housekeeper
A nanny
A secretary
Another set of arms
To get organized
Help

Other moms described the difference between expectations and reality: *I find myself screaming and getting frustrated and I know that's not what I'm supposed to be doing. Sometimes I feel like I'm losing my mind. I need help!*

While we might blurt out confessions like these, when it comes down to everyday life, most of us have a difficult time asking for help. Griping comes more easily. We whine and even scream on occasion. And many of us have mastered the martyr role, in which we carry on our work while sighing frequently and loudly, in hopes that someone will notice our weariness and step in to help. But when it comes to asking for specific assistance, we button our lips and shut in our discomfort.

✿ In the previous story, how do you think Susan got to such a state of frustration? List some factors below:

_____

_____

Some of us feel that asking for help is a sign of weakness, and we don't want to appear weak. As mothers, our jobs are to handle whatever comes with patience and immediate solutions. When a broken toy is tearfully brought to us, we glue it back together. When an outfit is soiled, we wash it. When the refrigerator is empty, we fill it. When the milk spills, we clean it up. It doesn't occur to some of us to enlist help until we're tied up in knots of legitimate commitments or completely out of gas, frustrated, and broken down with fatigue.

Further, we feel guilty about asking for help. Just admitting that we can't DO IT ALL and could use some help feels like admitting failure. Use a playpen. How could we? Let the baby cry? No way! Make a microwave dinner? Are you kidding? Mothers of preschoolers don't have occasional guilt. We have "perma-guilt," ever-present in the wear of life. If we don't "make it from scratch" every time, it doesn't count.

As much as we'd like to have some help and desperately need help, we refrain from actually asking for it. For some reason, the toughest question we may ever have to ask is: "Will you help me?"

Help Yourself

Learning to help yourself is the first step in conquering this need for help. Maybe you're a single mom and it's all you can do just to get the kids to day care, handle the day's work, and then get them back home and fed again in the evening. Or, maybe you're married, but your husband works long hours, or travels all week, or works nights, or simply isn't interested in his family role. "Help? Ha! Where can I go to find help?" you ask.

Partners in Parenting

Moms of young children need help from a myriad of sources. The Bible encourages us to turn to others: "Two are better than one, because they have a good return for their work: If one falls down, his friend can help him up. But pity the man who falls and has no one to help him up!" (Eccl. 4:9-10).

Who are your partners in parenting? your best friend? your husband? your doctor? your child's preschool teacher? a home-schooling networking group? a baby-sitter? your next-door neighbor? a grandmother? From extended family to the friends who have become your chosen family, to community and church resources, you have partners in parenting. Though a mother is always "on duty," she can partner with others to share the responsibility.

❀ Compile a list of your "partners in parenting." Write their names below:

_____

_____

Ask for Help.

Help is available. But we have to learn to help ourselves. We have to recognize and admit that sometimes we can't do it all. We don't have to feel guilty about appearing weak and admitting this normal need. But we do have to learn to ask—directly, using words. No one can read your mind. No one will simply waltz in and save you.

I needed to go to the dentist. My mother couldn't take care of the kids. I was used to handling things on my own and didn't want to ask my friend. But I had to .... and she didn't mind at all.

Remember that you weren't meant to be all things at all times to your children. That's not healthy for them or for us. Relinquish some control over some areas of responsibility. Share the load as well as the laurels. You may discover that you are not as indispensable as you thought, but you'll be more sane.

If you want help, if you truly want to share the load, ask for the help you need.

Friends as Helpers

When my toddler fell on the fireplace hearth, I panicked! My husband was at work and we were new in the neighborhood. What else could I do? I grabbed a towel and my child and ran next door. Thank goodness, my neighbor was home! She bundled up her little one and raced me to the emergency room.

A natural place to ask for help is to ask a friend. Mom and author Donna Partow confesses this slow but sure discovery in her book, *No More Lone Ranger Moms*: "This motherhood trip wasn't designed for lone rangers. It takes more than one woman against the world to raise a child in this increasingly complex and dangerous world. Even the pioneers sometimes circled the wagons. Women need one another. It's time to circle the wagons."[1]

One-on-One Help

When you finally get up the nerve to ask a friend for help, you may be pleasantly surprised by the response. The result of receiving help one-on-one outweighs the risk of asking. In fact, many long-lasting friendships begin this way.

Bartering: Trading Tasks

Bartering is an old-fashioned term to describe task-trading. Ideally, moms come together and meet their individual needs by swapping strengths. Bartering is a way to receive the help you need without spending the money you don't have. Bartering also makes it possible to spend more time on tasks you enjoy doing while allowing someone else to fill in on duties you don't enjoy as much. If you are a wallpaper whiz but hate to garden, swap talents with a neighbor. If you love to cook, but not with kids in the kitchen, arrange for a friend to watch all the kids while you cook for both families.

Support Groups

Support groups are for all sorts of people who come together to meet common needs. Mothers of young children especially benefit by forming or joining support groups.

I first came to MOPS (Mothers of Preschoolers) when a friend invited me. As I sat there with that group of women, I thought to myself, How pathetic. I'm at a support group. Have I really sunk this low? After I went through the complete session, I realized it was fun and exciting to learn in different areas and to help solve problems by sharing with other women.

Join a support group on parenting issues where you can learn from others struggling with the same questions and concerns. Friends, in a sense, are a support group. They offer comfort, a sense of community, and practical assistance.

✿ In the blanks, write the names of friends who fit each category:

1. Home during the day _____

2. Available evenings _____

3. Available weekends_____

4. Would trade baby-sitting with me _____

5. Would trade baby-sitting for a service I provide _____

6. Would join a baby-sitting coop _____

Husband Help

- If you're married, the most obvious source of help is your husband. But expecting help from him may not always be feasible.
  I'm married but sometimes feel like a single mom because my husband works 12 to 14 hours a day, 6 days a week.
- Or, maybe he's not aware that you could use some help.
  My kids place their food and drink orders all day. My husband comes home, eats, and goes to bed. I feel like no one thought of me at all the whole day.
- Or, maybe he doesn't understand the kind of help you need.
  When the kids whine and cry, my husband tells me not to let them get to me. He tells me what to do, instead of helping with them.
- Or, maybe you feel he works so hard that you shouldn't ask for his help at home. And when you do ask, you feel guilty. What about the issue of roles? What is the mom's job and what is the dad's? How do we sort through who does what?
  My husband comes home and my son wants Daddy. They play and have fun, and I feel invisible. I feel like I work all the time—if not with my son, then in the house. When my husband comes home from work, his job is done and playtime starts.
- Sometimes when you ask for help, you get no response. So rather than raise an issue, you do it yourself.
  One Saturday I was supposed to watch both kids, clean and vacuum, do the dishes and laundry, get dinner, and still have time to relax with my husband. It didn't work because he wouldn't help out. So I ended up doing everything myself.

Is it realistic to expect a dad to help? And if so, how do we translate these expectations into reality?

Sometimes I feel myself hitting my limit and know I need some help. I realize I need to ask for help and not feel bad about it, but I find it difficult to ask, especially when my husband has had a long week at work.

I feel so guilty asking for help. He has a full-time job, and mothering is my full-time job.

Clarify a Co-Parenting Partnership.

There are so many demands on our time that it feels like tag-team parenting. I watch our son while my husband works. My husband watches him while I fix dinner. I watch him while my husband mows the lawn. Now we're trying to make an effort to do this together.

In order to mother most effectively, we're wise to define what we expect the contribution of mothers and fathers to be in parenting. Are both parents? Are both parents responsible for the development and health of a child?

In her book, *Becoming a Woman of Strength*, Ruth Barton writes:

The most encouraging thing that has happened for me as a mother is that Chris (my husband) and I have begun seeing ourselves more clearly as a team in this challenge-of-a-lifetime called parenting. I have found that I do not need another book on how to be a better mother. ... What I have needed is my husband, the father of these children, to participate more fully with me in this great call of God upon our lives. I have needed to hear him say with words and with action, "You are not alone. These children are just as much my responsibility as they are yours."[2]

Research shows mothers and fathers parent in different ways and provide for unique needs in their children. Whereas the mother is the primary source of attachment necessary for infant bonding and future social relationships, the father is the main source for increasing the child's physical and intellectual independence.

Developing a co-parenting style requires honest self-examination and careful communication. If you're running the family ship like the captain of the fleet, issuing orders and demanding compliance, you may enjoy a sense of control, but you won't see help coming from your husband. A willingness to help comes from a shared sense of ownership of responsibility. Are your children your children or are they your husband's children as well?

Carefully observe your behavior for a few days. Do you leave detailed lists about how to diaper, feed, and play with the baby when you are away, or do you allow your husband the freedom to decide what works for him? When he's on duty with the children, do you label the activity baby-sitting or is it parenting? Baby-sitting implies he is temporarily assuming your responsibility, while parenting denotes shared responsibilities. Even subtle words like these can communicate that what he is doing as a father is not as meaningful as what you do as mother.

If we want help, we must examine our behaviors and be willing to make adjustments in order to create the potential for the co-parenting partnership.

♣ Find an appropriate time to discuss co-parenting with your husband. If you are in agreement about the concept, use the following sample and copy your co-parenting covenant on another piece of paper and sign it. Use it not as a weapon but rather as a working statement of your agreements in the parenting task.

Believing it to be God's will that we became one flesh in marriage and that God has blessed our union with a child(ren), and believing that God intends that both of us take an active role in the parenting responsibility,

*We, _____ and _____,
covenant to work together as a parenting team to provide for our children's nurture physically, intellectually, emotionally, and spiritually. We will seek to honor each other in decision-making and demonstrate value for each other by balancing responsibilities as much as possible.*

Specifically, we commit to sharing these parenting tasks: (list)

Each of us commits to taking major responsibility for these specific tasks:
    Husband   *Wife*

Ask Your Husband for Help.

If your sources of help include a husband, and you have clarified your co-parenting responsibilities, then ask him for help! Here's how:

- **Ask clearly and directly.** Don't hint. Don't sigh or pout. Don't expect him to read your mind or even notice your needs. Tell him. Put your request in words. *"I need help with the housework. Would you please vacuum for me?"* *"I need to go shopping. Would you please watch Rachel tonight while I go?"* *"I need help with grocery shopping this week. Would you be willing to go this time?"*

  If this is the first time you've asked your husband for help, choose a calm moment to do so. Resist the urge to strike out angrily in a moment of frustration or panic with accusations: "You never help!" Instead, at the beginning of a day that you know will be stressful, sit down and state your need clearly and without a lot of explanation, justification, or emotion.

- **Live with the results.** If you ask your husband to vacuum, resist the urge to critique his work. If you ask him to take Rachel while you shop, then embrace his choices as to what he does with her while you're away. If you send him to the grocery store, enjoy his purchases when he returns. The fact is clear: if you want help, receive it graciously in the form in which it comes. He may not do it exactly as you would, but criticizing his help may cause him to withdraw it altogether.

- **Risk.** It may appear risky to change a pattern of relating or communicating in a marriage. If your husband has grown accustomed to your being a

"Fathers, do not exasperate your children; instead, bring them up in the training and instruction of the Lord." Ephesians 6:4

"Supermom/Superwoman," he may have a hard time readjusting to your new requests for help. Give him time. Gently reassure him that you're not abdicating your nurturing role in the family, but that you are just recognizing your needs and limits and accepting the fact that you can't do it all.

🌼 Identify one task you want your husband to do. Answer these questions before you ask him for help.

1. What part of the job would you like him to do? _____

> When you invest yourself in a loving relationship, you can learn to ask for the help you need.

2. Depending on the task, can you accept a result that may be different from the way you would do it? ☐ Yes ☐ No
3. Are you willing for him to work on his own timetable? ☐ Yes ☐ No
   If not, when do you want the task accomplished?
4. When will you ask for more help? ☐ Today? ☐ Tomorrow?

Undoubtedly, there will be times when your husband will simply refuse your requests. Learn to respond without an emotional outburst. Receive his "No" the way you would want him to receive your "No." But don't stop asking. Find another opportunity when you need his help and ask again. Understand that husband help grows out of a growing relationship. When you invest yourself in a loving relationship, you can learn to ask for the help you need, and he can learn to offer it.

Mother's Little Helpers

How do you get your children to help? Some scoff at the mere thought. "I'd rather do it myself," most of us say, after nagging them unsuccessfully or refusing to live with the quality of results.

Others joke about the idea of motivating children to help out. It has been said that there are three ways to get something done: do it yourself, hire someone, or forbid your kids to do it. But there is another tactic. You can train your children to help. Through a deliberate choice of the will, careful follow-through, and much determination, you can turn your children into mother's little helpers.

Why Training Our Children to Help Is Good.

There are two reasons why training our children to help us is a good idea:

- Learning to help mom is good for children.
  In her book, *Do I Have To?* Patricia Sprinkle suggests that the "ultimate purpose of parenting is to help our children move out of our lives."[3] If she's right, then we'd better start empowering our preschool-aged children to begin to do for themselves now what they will need to do for themselves later.

Cooking, cleaning, and laundering skills must be taught by instruction and repetition. A child does not automatically begin to exercise these skills when he or she turns the age of 18. Further, the skills learned in one's nuclear family will be reflected in their future families and working relationships. What we teach our children now will make a difference in who they become later.

• Learning to help mom is good for mom.

Ah, to come home and find the table set! Or, to see a four-year-old struggle to make a bed and triumph in the result! To climb into a clean bathtub! Or, to discover cereal bowls in the dishwasher instead of on the table! Such help is good!

♣ Here are some cleaning games for preschoolers to play as you work together on projects around the house. When you have completed the game, give it a star rating (4 stars for "let's do this again" down to 1 star for "worked but not well").

____ 1. *Colors and Shapes:* Say to your child: "Let's pick up all the red toys. Now let's pick up the blue ones." Then "Let's pick up the squares and rectangles. Now the toys with round parts." Or, "Let's put all the glasses into the dishwasher. Now let's put in all the plates."

____ 2. *Observer Game:* Say, "You put away 10 things and let's see if I can remember them in order. Mary, put away a ball. Mary, put away a ball and a truck. Mary, put away a ball, a truck, and a doll."

____ 3. *Dust Muppet or Monster:* Draw a face on a large white sock for a dust mitt that "eats" dust.

____ 4. *Family Army Game:* Play march music, then march around the room picking up and putting away toys in time to the music.

____ 5. *Ant Legion:* Read aloud Proverbs 6:6-7. Talk about how hard ants work, then pronounce everyone an ant. Encourage ants to see how fast they can clean a room.

____ 6. *Do It with Me:* Say, "You make one side of the bed and I'll make the other." "You vacuum the room while I dust it." "You clean the mirror while I clean the sink." Tell jokes or stories while you work together.

____ 7. *Surprise Me!* A parent leaves the room after asking the child to see how much he or she can finish before the parent returns. The parent pops right back in and says, "I was just teasing this time, but you don't know when I'll be back next time, do you?" Return when you think the job may be complete.

____ 8. *"This Is the Way We ..."* Remember that old song? Sing together as you do the chore. Count how many times you sing it before the job is done.

____ 9. *Go Shopping.* Fill a wagon, buggy, or box with toys to be put away, pretending you are shopping. "Oh, I think I'll buy this bear. What will you buy?"

____ 10. *Beat the Clock:* Agree to work 10 minutes. Set a timer.[4]

"Go to the ant, you sluggard; consider its ways and be wise. It has no commander, no overseer or ruler, yet it stores its provisions in summer and gathers its food at harvest." Proverbs 6:6-7

How to Help Your Children Help

Obviously, we can't expect much in the way of help from children under the age of two. But even toddlers can begin to "help Mommy" with small tasks.

- Select age-appropriate tasks for your children. Chores can actually assist their feelings of doing things "all by themselves." Increasing responsibilities as the age of your children increases will keep them motivated and challenged.

- Motivate your children with rewards. Whether it's verbal praise, an allowance, or something else you choose, motivate your children to be helpers. Withhold rewards until tasks are complete; it teaches them about logical consequences. Once the tasks are satisfactorily completed, present the rewards with gusto!

- Adjust your standards of a job well-done. Children will often mess up more than they clean up as they learn the helping process. Steel yourself during these days. Your response to initial efforts will set the tone for future attempts. If a child feels unsuccessful, he or she may not want to risk a future failure. Reward the effort and the attitude more than the perfection of the task completed.

With patience and persistence, mother's little helpers can grow into mom's main helpers.

With patience and persistence, mother's little helpers can grow into mom's main helpers.

🍀 Patricia Sprinkle lists these age-appropriate tasks in her book, *Do I Have To?* Put a check by the tasks your children can successfully complete. Star those you intend to begin teaching this week.

Tasks for Two- and Three-Year-Olds

☐ Load spoons into dishwasher	☐ Help feed animals
☐ Put away toys after play	☐ Wipe table
☐ Dry unbreakable dishes	☐ Sweep (small broom)
☐ Stir orange juice	☐ Entertain infant
☐ Bring in newspaper	☐ Mop small area
☐ Pour milk (small pitcher)	☐ Empty wastebaskets
☐ Dust furniture	☐ Fold dishtowels
☐ Dig and pull weeds in garden	☐ Brush teeth, wash face
☐ Put away silverware	☐ Pick up trash in yard
☐ Unload clothes dryer	☐ Set table (from diagram)
☐ Wipe mirrors (parent sprays)	☐ Tidy magazines, sofa pillows
☐ Assist with stirring in cooking	☐ Dress and undress

Additional Tasks for Four- and Five-Year-Olds

☐ Put away clean clothes   ☐ Plant seeds

☐ Clean mirrors and glass alone   ☐ Mix salads

☐ Set a complete table   ☐ Grate cheese

☐ Clean bathroom sinks   ☐ Put away groceries

☐ Help with simple desserts   ☐ Sort clean laundry

☐ Help load dishwasher   ☐ Hang towels after bath

☐ Take dirty clothes to hamper   ☐ Carry own dishes to sink

☐ Bring in mail and put in proper place   ☐ Sort wash loads by color[5]

Helping Your Helpers

Whether you find help in your husband, a child, a day-care center, a school, or a church, learn the art of delegation. Delegation actually makes it possible to multiply your presence, your impact and your time while developing others' skills.

In her book, *Thriving as a Working Woman,* Gwen Ellis applies delegation principles from the working world to home life.

1. Decide what you want done. Set goals and make them measurable and specific.

2. If your needs or circumstances change, inform your helpers. For example, your baby-sitter needs to know if you're beginning to potty-train your toddler, along with some guidelines about the way you are approaching this challenge.

3. Pick the right person for the job.

4. Train the person for the job.

5. Check on your helper without hovering.

6. Be available for further training.

7. Give your helper the whole task. Resist the urge to go back in there and finish up once you've assigned a task.

8. Rotate the more disliked tasks among family members.

9. Keep cool when someone makes a mistake.[6]

If we want our helpers to be all the help they can be, we need to help them help!

❀ If you are still not convinced your children are part of the solution to your stressful lifestyle, repeat the *Mothering Maxim* on page 69 until you believe it!

Emotional Help

Sometimes when moms cry out for help, the need is not physical but emotional, and sometimes that need can't be met by those around us. Sometimes you will feel helplessly overwhelmed and wonder if you need professional help. How do you know?

First, be careful not to mistake a need for help as necessarily a need for professional help. "There's a great temptation to look at other people and think: 'She's got

"God collects all your tears. He knows all about you."
Psalm 56:8

two children and she can really handle it,'" Susan Yates admits. "'I'm about to die with one! What's wrong with me?' We are all made differently and we have different levels of cope-ability."[7]

How do you know if you've reached your limit of cope-ability? Most professionals agree that there are certain symptoms of psychological ill health:

- If you are in danger of hurting yourself or your children either verbally or physically, you need professional help.
- If you exhibit the symptoms of depression: loss or increase in appetite, apathy, increased or decreased sleep, you may need professional help.
- If you think you are addicted to drugs or alcohol, you need professional help.

Areas of professional input include self-development, marriage, sexual issues, childrearing, and physical issues. To find a professional who can be of help, contact your local church, your insurance company, or your medical doctor. Friends may also be a good source of referrals when your comfort level allows you to ask.

The Ultimate Helper

There is a greater and free source of help that's available to every mother of preschoolers, merely for the asking.

❀ Reread *This Week's Verse* on page 69. Say the verse several times until you can repeat it from memory. Consider writing the verse on index cards and posting them in several key places around your house.

"Very early in the morning, while it was still dark, Jesus got up, left the house and went off to a solitary place, where he prayed."
Mark 1:35

God is always present, ready to offer us the most consistent help we can find. When we turn to Him in prayer, He hears and responds with love and care. If Jesus needed to pray about His daily activities, how much more should we be committed to prayer as we begin each day.

Help is there for you, Mom. But getting help begins by identifying its sources and then learning to ask for it. That may feel uncomfortable at first, but the risk is worth the reward. Take the first step toward that goal today.

Recreation

Sometimes I Need a Break

Eighteen-month-old Scott whimpered as Lynne lifted him from the crib and pressed his feverish forehead to her cheek. She'd been up with him most of the night and knew he needed to see the doctor. He clung to her neck—a hot, sweaty body in his footie jammies—as she dialed the phone number and made an appointment for an hour later. Mentally, she began to rearrange her day.

"Stephen!" she called to her older son. "You need to get dressed. We have to take Scott to the doctor!" Now that he was four, Stephen could at least dress himself, but he'd have to miss preschool this morning. And now she wouldn't be able to do the family bills for Jeff today as she'd promised.

At the doctor's office, Lynne read to Stephen while trying to comfort Scott on her lap. She touched his flushed cheeks and guessed that his temperature was soaring. Sure enough. A few minutes later, the doctor diagnosed another ear infection—his third in six months.

Lynne gratefully took the prescription slip, zipped Scott and Stephen into their coats, loaded up her diaper bag and purse, and headed to the car.

When they pulled into the grocery store parking lot, Scott started to cry. "Honey, hang on," she said soothingly. "Mommy's going to get you some medicine." He quieted as she lifted him into her arms, took Stephen's hand and walked into the store.

"It'll be about 20 minutes," the pharmacist told her. Great. How was she going to keep two little kids happy in the aisles of a grocery store? Her head began to ache. *I can do this*, she told herself calmly.

This Week's Verse

"Come to me, all you who are weary and burdened, and I will give you rest. Take my yoke upon you and learn from me, for I am gentle and humble in heart, and you will find rest for your souls. For my yoke is easy and my burden is light."
Matthew 11:28-30

Mothering Maxim
If Mama ain't happy, ain't nobody happy.

Forty-five minutes later, Lynne finally arrived back home, heated soup for Stephen and coaxed a few bites down Scott, followed by his medicine. At last, she rocked Scott to sleep and settled Stephen down with a video.

Now I can get something done, she thought as she sat down at the kitchen table with her calculator. Then she noticed a big mess on the carpet in the next room.

Dog throw up! She jumped up, grabbed a wad of paper towels, hauled out the vacuum, and returned to the mess. But as she flicked the switch, the vacuum hissed and stopped. She recognized that sound ... a broken belt.

She marched back to the closet to get a new belt. When she returned to the defunct vacuum, she turned it upside down and plopped down on the floor. Right beside the dog mess.

Hastily, she pulled at the steel belt cover, but it wouldn't budge. Suddenly, it was all too much for her. She had nothing left. Hot tears ran down her face, taking her mascara with them. *Good grief! I can make it through a whole night with a sick child, a doctor's visit, and a half-hour delay at the pharmacy, but I fall apart because I can't fix a broken vacuum belt!*

"Mom! The movie's over!" called Stephen from the other room. "Now what do I do?"

"What do *I* do?" Lynne cried. "I need a break!" But no one responded.

Always on Duty

Even if I'm over at a friend's house having coffee, I can "hear" my children. Even when I'm asleep, I'm still listening for them. There is no time when I am "off duty."

This mom is not alone. Most moms of young children report that it is not a single major crisis that brings them to the edge of breakdown. Rather, it is the constant accumulation of everyday hassles with no breaks. It's also the constant drive to live up to expectations: "Cleanliness is next to godliness." "Don't put off to tomorrow what you can do today." "Don't play until your work is done." Women hear these ditties from the time they are small children. Added to the list for moms of preschoolers are such condemning prescriptives as: "But your child needs you!"

Moms of preschoolers are said to be the most exhausted, fatigued, and worn-out strata of our society. Functioning on little sleep, unbalanced nutrition, little exercise, and frazzled nerves, we're expected to constantly juggle a jumble of balls without ever dropping one or losing our footing.

✿ Estimate the number of hours you spend per week in "mothering" responsibilities. *Circle your estimate.*   *under 20*   *20-40*   *40-60*   *more than 60*

Often, the cycle of exhaustion intensifies as moms push themselves harder and harder to perform better and better. "Chronically tired women exhibit sluggishness, impatience, depression, irritability, and emotional outbursts," writes Dolores Curran. "They aren't easy to live with, even with themselves. And they don't like their lives very much. Often the fatigued woman tries to do more than less, feeling that renewed activity will reduce her tiredness."[1]

No kidding! We're worn out! Wrung out! Sucked dry! The unceasing needs, the responsibility, the pressure to be all our children need.

Everyone But Mom

Kids play. Dads channel surf. Even grandmas and grandpas enjoy the whimsical, more carefree stuff of life. But a mom is constantly surrounded by her responsibilities, and that means work, work, work.

- Anne Morrow Lindbergh talks about this pressure and how a woman gives herself away without taking time for replenishment:

  All her instinct as a woman—the eternal nourisher of children, of men, of society— demands that she give. Her time, her energy, her creativeness drain out into these channels if there is any chance, any leak. Traditionally we are taught, and instinctively we long, to give where it is needed—and immediately. Eternally, woman spills herself away in driblets to the thirsty, seldom being allowed the time, the quiet, the peace, to let the pitcher fill up to the brim.[2]

- But here's the perplexing part: While the need for a break is universally expressed, the habit of taking time for recreation is almost nonexistent. Moms need a break, but they don't take it. Sometimes we don't take breaks because we're uncertain about leaving our children.

  Leaving my children has always been very traumatic. They seem to get thrown off schedule and are extremely clingy when I return. What if my children need me and I'm not there?!

- Others "break not" because of some belief that it's lazy or selfish to kick back.

  I don't take breaks and don't realize I need to until I am unkind and unreasonable. Then my husband says, "You need a break." Why can't I sense that before it's too late?

- To this excuse, Dr. Holly Atkinson responds that most women have been reared to believe their needs should come last: "A woman is trained to be self-sacrificing. To get through her list of things to do, she first sacrifices her free time. Then she sacrifices her sleep."[3]

  I keep thinking I can stay up late to get time for myself. But I'm not as young as I used to be and it just ends up making me more tired and grumpy!

Moms of preschoolers have a basic, undeniable need to take a break before they break. To come apart before they come apart. To play. To recreate.

The first few weeks after my son was born, I would have given anything to have my old life back again ... to take a nap on Sunday afternoon, to go camping on the spur of the moment, or go out without worrying about a baby-sitter. I didn't expect such a constant weight of responsibility— with no breaks.

✿ Where are you on the "break" or "break not" polarity? Check the statement that is true for you.

☐ I'm one of the "break not" tired and grumpy moms!

☐ I take breaks but I usually feel guilty.

☐ Are you kidding? Where's the party? I'm there!

☐ Other? _____

Re-Creation

"Where freedom of play has been lost," writes Jurgen Moltman in *The Theology of Play*, "the world turns into a desert." Too many mothers of preschoolers live a desert life. What is needed is space—both a time and a place—to recreate. To re-create who we are and what we have to offer others.

The word *re-create* actually means "to restore, refresh, or create anew" and can mean "to restore in body or mind especially after work, by play, amusement or relaxation." What moms of young children need is re-creation!

Re-Creation Makes Us Better.

A recent *McCall's* survey reports that women are two to four times more likely than men to suffer from nightmares, upset stomachs, and feelings of being overwhelmed and depressed. Eighty-three percent of the women surveyed feel pressure to be the best in everything they do.

Re-creation renews us. "Leisure ... is a point of contact with reality and a catalyst for new experiences, new people, and new places," writes Tim Hansel in his book, *When I Relax, I Feel Guilty.* "The gift of wholeness again becomes a hope and a possibility."[4]

> It is really nice to get out without the children and talk to people my age or just do something I want. When I come back home, I feel better. I'm back on track with my kids as far as patience and understanding go.

Re-Creation Makes Us Better Moms.

Who among us doesn't want to be a better mom? We weigh our efforts and wonder how to improve our impact on our kids. A study at the universities of Utah and Wisconsin reveals that stress (including daily maternal hassles) causes more interference in the relationship between a mother and her child than a job.[5]

When we take a break to make ourselves better, we become better moms. As Dolores Curran puts it, "Taking a break is not selfish but self-preserving."[6] And pastor's wife, Denise Turner, has also learned this truth: "A long time passed before I realized the ability to enjoy my children is closely dependent upon the amount of time I am spending having fun with my husband and having fun by myself."[7]

The fact is that caring for our own needs better equips us to meet the needs of those who depend on us. Taking time for recreation communicates to others, our families especially, that we recognize the value of taking care of ourselves.

> I'm at my most self-disciplined and patient best when I have chosen time for prayer, a walk, and some reading in the morning.

❀ Reread the *Mothering Maxim* on page 81. Does it describe reality at your house?

☐ Yes ☐ No

Check the statement below that describes you:

☐ *I will do what it takes to be a happier person!*
☐ *I don't see how I can be happy under my present circumstances.*

If the family's happiness depends—at least partially—on your happiness, then make a commitment to improving your happiness quotient.

So how do we learn to take a break and enjoy the benefits it offers?

Play School

Most of us have to learn how to play. We figured it out as children, of course, but as we head into our adult years, we outgrow the habit of playing, just as we outgrow items of clothing. As adults, play means getting in touch with the childlikeness we've left behind. Several ingredients go into play. We can learn to enjoy them individually or in combination.

My husband and I hadn't been out alone together for almost a year. On our big night out we went shopping for a mattress. We were so excited—we had a blast!

Learn to Laugh.

When we can laugh at life and at ourselves as we muddle through it, we are happier, saner, and even more physically fit. Laughter eases strain and relaxes tension. According to some studies, it exercises the abdomen, increases circulation, and improves muscle tone. It's been said that laughing heartily several times a day has the same benefits as 10 minutes of vigorous exercise. So let's get started!

Laughing at ourselves takes the sting out of our mistakes as well as those things we simply can't control. Since we have to live with ourselves, we might as well be good company. Humor also helps us to get a grip on situations in which we tend to lose our temper.

"The mother who can laugh at herself, with her children, and at the impossible situations of life, is far ahead on the road to personal control," write Grace Ketterman and Pat Holt in their book, *When You Feel Like Screaming*. "Having the wisdom to step back and see the humor ... helps (us) gain control."[8] Laughter gives us perspective.

Interestingly, laughter and leisure combine to alleviate stress and its ill-effects. When Norman Cousins faced a serious illness, he used the therapy of laughter in his recovery. Ten-minute daily doses of *Candid Camera* and *The Marx Brothers* taken from his hospital bed eased his pain and helped him to sleep well.

Laughter is contagious. Someone once said, "Smile awhile and while you smile, another smiles and soon there are miles and miles of smiles because you smiled." Your facial expression is contagious, so smile to yourself, smile at your kids, and smile

I agree to play hide-and-seek with the kids—they hide, and I get all the peace I want whenever I want until I choose to find them!

at others—at stoplights, in the mall, or anywhere. When you wear a smile across your face, it's not as easy to feel growly and grouchy.

William Arthur Ward put it in a nutshell when he wrote: "A keen sense of humor helps us overlook the unbecoming, to understand the unconventional, to tolerate the unpleasant, to overcome the unexpected, and to outlast the unbearable."[9]

I awoke one morning to find my children sitting in a mound of Cheerios® on the floor. They were so thrilled about fixing breakfast— I had to laugh!

✿ Adapt these suggestions from Barbara Johnson. Check the ones that describe your usual approach to life:

☐ 1. Try to see the humor in a situation around you. (Example in the margin)
☐ 2. Imagine how a child might view your situation.
☐ 3. Play ... with kids, dogs, cats, kites, whatever.
☐ 4. When in doubt, go for the goofy.
☐ 5. Browse the comedy aisle at the video store.
☐ 6. Spend time with friends who make you chuckle.[10]

Lighten Up.

What's the big deal? Why do we take so many things so seriously when they aren't that important? For example, we need to ask ourselves what's more important—tucking a happy, grubby child into bed or a clean, cranky one?

We need to bring spontaneity back into our routine occasionally. We assume that a trip outside the front door requires the accompaniment of armloads of equipment. But does it really? What would happen if we had only one diaper, some wipes, and a bottle of juice in our possession at any given moment? What if—instead of fretting over the pile of Legos® littering our living room floor—we got down among them and saw life from the perspective of a two-year-old? Did you ever notice how many exciting stimuli lie just six inches off the floor?

I got so tired of being late during the days of potty-training. So I put the potty chair in the minivan and strapped my little guy in!

Re-creation requires spontaneity. Don't put your life on hold during these days filled with opportunities to make memories with your little ones. How about breaking your schedule for some unplanned fun? What if—on a clear summer night—you woke your child and took her stargazing? Embrace fun wherever and whenever it comes, and enter into it wholly.

When his son was getting ready to begin college life, H. Jackson Brown jotted down a few words of wisdom to send with him. Brown didn't know then that all over America people would take his advice to heart when he wrote his best-selling *Life's Little Instruction Book.*

✿ Check off Brown's quick, easy, and inexpensive suggestions as you complete each one. Attempt at least one a day if possible:

- ☐ 3. Watch a sunrise.
- ☐ 11. Sing in the shower.
- ☐ 69. Whistle.
- ☐ 182. Be romantic.
- ☐ 244. Buy a bird feeder and place it where it can be seen from your kitchen window.
- ☐ 246. Wave at children on school buses.
- ☐ 267. Lie on your back and look at the stars.
- ☐ 330. Rekindle an old friendship.
- ☐ 337. Reread your favorite book.
- ☐ 345. Try everything offered by supermarket food demonstrators.
- ☐ 347. Tell someone you love them.
- ☐ 376. Save an evening a week for just you and your spouse.
- ☐ 402. Begin each day with your favorite music.
- ☐ 477. Give thanks before every meal.
- ☐ 510. Count your blessings.[11]

Slow Down.

What's the hurry? In his book, *The Hurried Child*, David Elkind cautions us to slow down our lives and our mothering. We're racing ourselves and our children past the very work of play they need to do in childhood.

Six-month-old babies are learning to sit, not run. Eighteen-month-olds move away from Mom and then back again every few minutes as they journey out to explore their worlds, while making sure she's close by. Three-year-olds want to touch, see, and do everything all by themselves and are frustrated if they can't.

Childhood comes with its specific tasks of accomplishment. Among them is play. In fact, a child's work is play. Through play, children internalize their personhood, sexuality, and understanding about life. When we forget either our children's need to play or our own, we forfeit the joy of living life as it was intended to be lived.

Slow down. Savor where you are. Believe it or not, this season shall pass. Quickly.

I desperately need time for myself time to just relax, be myself, recharge my battery, so I can make it to the weekend when my husband will be home.

Physical Fitness Fun

Doctors, psychologists, and other experts knowingly tout the benefits of physical fitness on general well-being. Bottom-line, when we're out of shape, we don't feel good and tire easily. In short, we're wretched to live with!

The break many moms need is a walk around the block to feel the fresh air and get the blood flowing. Some need better nutrition—something other than leftover

I never get any
exercise. And my
exhaustion overcomes
my enthusiasm.

I used to play tennis
and be active, but now
I'm out of shape.

peanut-butter-and-jelly sandwiches and Cheerios®. Others need to lie down for a half-hour nap each day. All these ingredients contribute to physical fitness.

While it's sometimes next to impossible to get that needed break, you can learn to take advantage of odd moments here and there.

❀ If you're a new mom with little time on your hands, use these ideas to help snatch a quick exercise session. Underline the ones that would work for you:
- Go for a jog and listen to a cassette or pray while you pound the pavement.
- While your tot naps, rake leaves, shovel snow, sweep the driveway, or do other calorie-burning yard work with a monitor close at hand.
- Join a health club that provides child care while moms work out.
- Take your baby on long walks in the stroller, or buy a three-wheeled jog stroller.
- Buy a baby tote for biking.
- Set up a schedule with another new mom who wants to work out. She keeps the babies for an hour while you exercise; then you keep them while she exercises.
- Hide your husband's golf clubs so you can step out and exercise while he keeps the kids for an hour or two on the weekend.
- Hire a baby-sitter while you work out—a healthy body and less-stressed mind is worth the few bucks.
- Exercise to a TV workout show, buy a few exercise videos, or rent your favorite celebrity's workout video to use while baby naps.[12]

Need to cultivate better nutritional habits? Diet with some pals. "Just say no to one temptation a day. Don't eat leftovers off the children's plates. Give up sugar for one weekend. Check out the fat grams for one meal. Stop snacking. Include more fruits and vegetables in the family menu. (The recommended quota is five servings a day.) Enlist the children's help in peeling oranges or tearing lettuce. Often when a child becomes a part-time chef, he or she will be more interested in tasting new creations.

❀ The following habits will help create a healthy lifestyle. Check the ones that characterize your lifestyle. Put a star beside those you want to become a habit:
- Eat breakfast.
- Drink eight glasses of water a day.
- Eat a healthy diet, including:
  — five servings of vegetables or fruits every day;
  — iron- and calcium-rich foods such as lean meats and green, leafy vegetables, including a vitamin supplement if necessary;
  — foods low in fat, high in protein and carbohydrates.

Be intentional about getting more rest. When you lay your little one down for a nap, lie down yourself. If your child has outgrown naps, maintain the regular quiet time and use that time to lie down together and read. No, you won't get the next load of wash folded, but you might be much easier to live with!

For many of us with overcrowded schedules, physical fitness is one of the first things to go. We figure no one will notice. Wrong. Whether or not the lack of love for our bodies shows on the outside, the inside suffers. And eventually, the damage will be demonstrated in the form of impatience, irritability, and general grouchiness. If a woman doesn't feel good about herself, she's less likely to treat others with goodness.

Getting into shape often takes discipline and determination, but the results are worthwhile and the process—once under way—can be fun. A bonus: exercise is addictive. Some advice? Just do it!

❀ Here's a Six-Week Starter Program that will reduce stress and tension and help you to look and feel better fast.

Weeks 1, 2, and 3:

- Walk outside, or get on your exer-cycle, stair-climber, or treadmill for 15 minutes, three times a week.
- Don't worry about distance or pace; focus solely on getting in 15 minutes of exercise time.
- Move your legs fast enough to increase your breathing rate, but not so fast that you become breathless. Maintain a steady comfortable pace throughout your exercise period.
- Exercise before breakfast or before dinner. (Indoor exercisers can watch TV or read while they exercise.)

Week 4: Exercise for 20 minutes, three times a week.

Week 5: Exercise for 25 minutes, three times a week.

Week 6: Exercise for 30 minutes, three times a week.

After Week 6:

- Either gradually increase time to 45 or 60 minutes, or you can gradually increase your pace within the 30-minute time frame.
- Walkers can alternate brisk walking with slow jogging (fast jogging and running increase your risk for injury).
- Indoor exercisers can increase the tension on their exercise equipment.
  Note: If you're trying to lose excess weight, consider getting a minimum of 35 minutes of brisk exercise every day.

Do you think this plan would work for you?　☐ Yes　☐ No

Feed Your Spirit

When I resigned from my management job to be a full-time homemaker, I expected to finally have more time to pray and read. Was I ever wrong! I have less time for myself. I no longer get breaks and no lunch hour to do with as I please!

When you think of taking a break, include a practice that will feed your spirit. During the days when we are giving on demand, we need a constant source of nourishment for ourselves as well.

Psalm 42:1-4 provides a mental picture of the many moms who'd love to spend time with God but can't seem to fit it into their hectic days: "As the deer pants for streams of water, so my soul pants for you, O God. My soul thirsts for God, for the living God. When can I go and meet with God?"

There are many days when our spirits feel parched and we wonder when—or if—we'll ever "meet with God" again. Even getting to church once a week is often difficult. Instead of waiting to go to the "house of the Lord," why not invite Him to your house? Sit down during a child's nap time and read a few verses from the Gospel of John. Use a mealtime blessing to pray about what's happened that day. Leave your Bible open on the table and read a phrase from one of the psalms as you walk by. Throughout the day graze on Scripture morsels from a flip book on the kitchen counter. Listen to a tape of the New Testament in the car.

❀ Take a prayer walk through the neighborhood. As you pass each house, pray for those who live there. If you don't know their names, God does! Better yet, He knows their needs!

Focus on Fun

We have a barn, horses, and a lot of hay bales. When I need some peace, I announce that I need to go out and restack the hay, but I really just go and sit on them. I can usually get 30 minutes out of this excuse and {my husband} never says anything to me about the messy barn!

Re-creation happens when we commit ourselves to focusing on fun, both for ourselves and for our family.

Mom Fun

Every mom needs something that is enjoyable for herself alone. Plan creatively to take a break by yourself. It might be only "Five Minutes of Peace," carved out of a quick trip to the supermarket or while running an errand. One mom describes her habit of "Wal-Marting":

Wal-Marting goes something like this: My day has gotten progressively worse. Any slight deviation from routine sets off my temper. My children seem particularly fussy. We run out of juice midday. The kitten keeps using the couch as a scratching post. Two unexpected bills come in the mail, and I get four phone calls during nap time. I can hardly wait for my husband to get home from work. As he walks through the door and asks me how my day has been, I explain that I am in need of some alone time. He says he'll see me later. I hop in the car and head to Wal-Mart.[13]

Your time alone might come through a scheduled breakaway. Many moms plan regular times for themselves. A craft or cooking class. A night out with the girls.

Expose yourself to new people and places. Take a day trip to an ethnic neighborhood. Read up on the culture and customs of other countries. Dine at ethnic eateries.

Develop a hobby. Think back over your life to the hobbies of your childhood. Pull out the stamp collection or the crafts from camp that excited you. Sign up at a community college for a class in pottery, painting, or woodworking. Consider joining a book club that reads and reviews current bestsellers in a small-group atmosphere. Spend time outdoors gardening. Pick up some gourmet skills in a cooking class.

Setting aside the time to fix your hair and makeup isn't always easy with small children underfoot, but once done, it goes a long way toward making your days go more smoothly.

"A cheerful look brings joy to the heart."
Proverbs 15:30

Everyone's beautiful in her own way, so think positively when you look into the mirror. Stand up straight and tighten your abdominals—this forces you into an upright position and into a more positive attitude. Try a little of the unabashed admiration that your toddler uses when he looks at himself in the mirror. Do not be preoccupied with your flaws.

Remember the words of Abe Lincoln upon overhearing someone remark that he was a "common-looking man": "Friend, the Lord prefers common-looking people. That is the reason he makes so many of them."[14]

Here are some beautiful ideas for at-home maintenance:

- Find a flattering hair style, then maintain it.
- Spend a little time planning your outfits. Get rid of the outdated garments from your closet so that you're not tempted to wear them.
- Invite a friend over and give each other a make-over. Solicit feedback on a potential new hairdo or make-up approach.

"A happy heart makes the face cheerful."
Proverbs 15:13

- If you love to keep up with fashion trends, read women's magazines for new hair and makeup techniques and fashion ideas.
- Don't abandon the little self-pampering luxuries you enjoyed before you had kids. Put someone else in charge of the real world while you take time out for a soaking bath. Then give yourself a manicure and pedicure, tweeze your eyebrows, and condition your hair. Treat yourself to a facial mask. Put wet tea bags over your eyes to remove puffiness.

Are you asking, *When would I have time for that?* Ask your husband for help, or if you're single, swap kids with another single mom. But deliberately set aside time for renewal. Then take action to ensure you use it. You'll find refreshment both in the anticipation and in the experience itself.

Family Fun

My son, to be kind to me one day, helped me with several chores. We did laundry together, swept floors, put away toys, and on and on. Later that day, he said we hadn't had any time for fun. My goals were met, but my son wanted my time and laughter more than anything. Now we set aside a day just for the "fun" stuff.

Dolores Curran, in her book *Traits of a Healthy Family*, lists a sense of play and humor as an important ingredient of a happy, balanced family. Some moms already know that family fun matters. As moms, we need to learn to make time for family fun. If we don't plan to play, it usually won't happen.

"Most middle-class Americans tend to worship their work, to work at their play, and to play at their worship," writes Gordon Dahl. "Their relationships disintegrate faster than they can keep them in repair, and their lifestyles resemble a cast of characters in search of a plot."[15]

❀ Underline the suggestions for family fun that would work for you:
- *Hold a family forum.* Allow each family member to select a fun activity for the month. Set the tone by being enthusiastic about the prospect. Include yourself in the decision-making process. You, too, should take a turn at creating fun.
- *View your family members as fun.* Instead of choosing activities that cost or purchasing amusements, think of the folks around you as a free source of fun. Play "Guess what animal I am?" or decorate each other with paper, tinsel, foil, or wrapping paper.
- *Celebrate the daily as well as the sensational.* Designate a dinner plate as a "Very Special Person Plate" and serve a meal on it to a family member in honor of an achievement or special occasion. Pull out all the stops on birthdays using balloons, homemade cards, birthday serenades at the exact moment of birth, and birthday crowns. Underline the value of each person in your family by singling out special days and moments to celebrate.
- *Keep traditions.* Every family has a few rituals they have "always" observed. Combine the memorable ones from your background with some from your husband's background, and then invent some new ones. Rituals offer meaning, predictability, and a heritage of values.

❀ List at least one family ritual that you observe. If you know where or when it began, tell the story. Be prepared to share it at your next group meeting.

_____

_____

Moms of preschoolers are among the most needy when it comes to recreation. We need to cultivate the habits of learning to laugh, lightening up, slowing down, and having fun. Take a break ... before you break!

Week 8

Perspective

Sometimes I Lose My Focus

D ebbie stood at the kitchen sink, gazing out the window daydreaming. Then, snapping back to reality, she remembered the water gushing from the faucet and began rinsing the breakfast dishes. Next, she wiped milk stains and sticky crumbs from the counter and swept the floor. Glancing into the family room, her next task loomed before her—cleaning the carpet littered with puzzle pieces, a plastic tea set, clothes, and crayons. Someday her kids would be grown and she would live in a house without clutter!

Just then she felt a tug on her jeans and looked down.

"Mommy, can you read to me?" four-year-old Shannon pleaded, clutching her favorite book, *Goodnight Moon.* Debbie had read that book to Shannon hundreds of times in the past few weeks.

"Not now, honey." Debbie sighed. "Maybe later."

Shannon whined and then collapsed at her mother's feet, gluing Debbie in place.

"Shannon! Can't you see that Mommy is very busy today? I have to finish cleaning the kitchen, wash clothes, and finish writing those thank-you notes for the presents we got when Meagan was born! And now you've made a huge mess in the family room, and I have to clean that up too!"

"But Mommy—the kitchen *is* clean! And you always wash clothes .... and the carpet doesn't look messy to me." Shannon pleaded.

"Not now, Shannon. Maybe later," Debbie firmly repeated as she pried the child's arms from her legs and marched to the washing machine. She had only a few towels to fold, but Debbie wasn't one to let them sit.

This Week's Verse
"Seek first his kingdom and his righteousness, and all these things will be given to you as well."
Matthew 6:33

Mothering Maxim
Fit today into the
BIGGER PICTURE of life.

The phone rang. It was her dear friend and former coworker, Beth. After chatting about 15 minutes, Debbie went to check on napping Meagan. Good, still asleep.

But where had Shannon gone? Peeking around the corner into her daughter's bedroom, Debbie found Shannon sitting in her pint-sized rocking chair, holding a book and facing a row of attentive stuffed animals arranged audience-style.

"In the great, green room, there was a telephone and a red balloon and a picture of a cow jumping over the moon. And there were three little bears sitting on chairs." Debbie listened as Shannon "read" from *Goodnight Moon*, mimicking her mother's voice.

Suddenly she snapped the book shut and announced to her eager audience, "I don't have time to read today! I have too much to do!" Rising quickly from her rocker, she marched over to a doll, picked her up, and then plopped her down in a playpen. "No, I can't read to you now. Maybe later. And don't ask me again! Can't you see I am busy?"

Debbie leaned against the hall wall and pondered the role-play she'd just observed. *Ouch! Is that really how Shannon sees me? From the mouth of a four-year-old! I guess I sometimes forget what's important and lose my focus.*

Another Perspective

Not now, maybe later. It's tough to hear that familiar mother-to-child answer and not feel a few pangs of guilt, isn't it? But this chapter isn't about guilt. It's about a larger struggle that we face day in and day out. The struggle to cope with our busyness and find focus, or perspective. The struggle to balance the urgent and the important. The struggle to recognize our choices and make them with wisdom so that we're less likely to experience regret or feel guilty.

What do we mean by "perspective"? Perspective is the ability to stand between yesterday and tomorrow and understand how and where today fits in. As the mothers of young children seeking to discover how our "todays" fit into our lifetime roles as women, we have to stand back and get a larger view of the whole of life. We have to identify goals that transcend today and remember what we're aiming toward.

I'm surprised I get so upset about unimportant things like a spilled drink.

Perspective means looking beyond the moment with a view toward the whole of life. And moms of preschoolers need perspective as they move through days in which the goal of a clean house can take precedence over tickle-wars, and completing a to-do list may win out over lap time.

Living with perspective is difficult at any stage of life. The present is so demanding that it takes on meaning of its own, separate from its rightful place in the context of forever. But for the mother of preschoolers, several mothering myths worm their way into our thinking and distort our focus.

Mothering Myths and Reality

Often we swallow certain mothering myths as truths, unaware that these falsehoods direct much of our thinking as well as our actions. As a result, we may forget why we're doing what we're doing and what really matters in the long run.

Following are four myths coupled with their corresponding realities. Read carefully to discover where you might be misled in what motivates your mothering.

Myth #1
If you control everything, life works.

Reality: You can't control everything. You have to go with the flow.

Exactly. The myth that we can make life work by being in control gives way to the reality that most of life is beyond our control. Trying to take charge of all events in life only leads to frustration and despair.

The hardest part of being a mother is not being able to control what another human being does.

The reality is that life has a life of its own. Take children, for instance. Babies spit up on you just as you're ready to walk out the door. Toddlers wet their training pants three weeks after you thought they'd mastered toilet-training. Kindergartners shyly hang back from their mothers on the first day of school, even though they've been impatiently checking off the days on a calendar for the past month.

Besides children, there is the everyday stuff of life that refuses our commands. Cars stall in traffic. Lines are long at the store. A filling breaks in a tooth. A button pops off a shirt. How do we handle the shattering of this myth of control? With a strong dose of practical action.

- *Relinquish control.* The Serenity Prayer, often quoted by persons dealing with addictions, also speaks powerfully to the world of the mother of preschoolers. Read the unforgettable words of Reinhold Neibuhr that appear in the margin.

God, grant me the serenity to accept the things I cannot change, the courage to change the things I can, and the wisdom to know the difference.

❀ What are some of your greatest fears as a mother?

_____

What are some of your greatest frustrations? _____

_____

Now go back through your responses and circle those that you can control! Moms who give over control to God report peace and rest.

- *Respond only to the responsibility you've been given.* So many of us borrow burdens from others. We decide we're responsible for a friend's happiness, for a child's health, for a husband's fulfillment.

Dr. Marianne Neifert, otherwise known as "Dr. Mom," admits candidly: "I can say: God didn't put all that stuff in my sack. When I looked inside, I saw my ambition, need for other people's approval, perfectionism. Those things were put there by me. That's why my sack was too heavy."[1]

Along these same lines, A. J. Russell, in his book, *God Calling*, suggests that stress results from carrying two days' burdens in one day. His words echo those of Jesus: "Therefore do not worry about tomorrow, for tomorrow will worry about itself. Each day has enough trouble of its own" (Matt. 6:34).

- *Humor helps.* When the myth that we can control life around us shatters, humor helps. Try these lines:

> *God put me on earth to accomplish a certain number of things.*
> *Right now I am so far behind, I will never die.*
> *Just when you thought you were winning the rat race, along come faster rats.*

Learn to smile at your inability to control. Humor eases our hurts or frustrations as we admit our humanity!

OK. Are you ready to shatter another myth?

Myth #2
I should do it all right and all right now.
Reality: I can't do it all, but I can do what's important.

Our expectations for ourselves and what we should be accomplishing are astronomically high and unrealistic. We've moved past the Supermom syndrome and climbed atop a pedestal of perfection. We assume that we should be able to do it all right and all right *now!*

Right? Wrong.

"As challenges keep coming," Erma Bombeck once said, "mothers realize they can't possibly keep pace or they'll wind up comatose in the kitchen sink."

We can fight against this second myth by taking deliberate steps to define and embrace what really matters in life.

- *Keep the main thing the main thing.* For moms of preschoolers, perspective comes as we define what really matters in mothering. Perspective is restored when we define for ourselves just what it is that we're trying to accomplish as mothers.

God has taught me to wait on Him as our military orders changed six times, as my husband decided to find work outside of the military, and as we lived in a state of limbo. All of this is very much against my nature. I am a planner, goal-oriented, compulsive organizer, and perfectionist.

An unexpected visitor drops by and I'm so embarrassed by the exposure of my lack of orderliness.

✿ For the following choices, underline the words that mean the most to you:

a clean home or a kind heart   good manners or good values

attitudes or appearance   quiet play or creativity

- *Allocate the investment of your time and energy based on the "main thing."* This myth of doing it all right and doing it all right now leads us to pay too much attention to the niggling little details of life. When we define for ourselves what really matters, we can then use such a definition as a measuring stick of our activities. Where are we spending our energies?

   Admittedly, there are times when it's tough to know whether or not an issue falls under "the main thing."

   Just when I think it's OK to go through the day in sweats, wear no makeup, and let the house look less than perfect while I spend time nurturing and playing with my children (who won't be children forever) ... and that it's OK not to look perfect (flat stomach, pre-pregnant weight, hair curled), my husband returns home from work with a comment about the house being a mess or dinner not being on the table or "What did you do all day and what's wrong with your hair?"

   Even when you communicate with your husband and agree upon values, ticklish spots remain.

I need to be flexible. Trying to stick to my own agenda causes 80 percent of our family's hassles.

✿ Think of a task that looms in front of you today. Ask yourself these questions: "Will it matter in five years?" and "What would happen if I ignored this issue?"

If the task does not make the "main thing" to-do list, what might be a better way to use your time?

_____

   Such questions provide the parameters we need to keep our focus. Here's a third mothering myth. See if you can relate.

Myth #3
The best way to make it through mothering is to
grin and bear it until it gets better.

Reality: Enjoy today. Make the most of life's irretrievable moments ... now.

How much of mothering do we miss because our focus is simply on making it through? Sure, we all seethe in the face of well-intentioned advice from kindly grandmothers in grocery stores who tell us (as we wrestle with three cranky kids in the checkout line): "These are the best days of your life! Enjoy them because they pass so quickly!"

   "Not quickly enough," we mutter under our breath.

   But these women do have a point—one that comes with the wisdom of their years. The stage of mothering young children is a *stage*. It only *feels* like an era! And it will pass. It will not last forever. It will end one day.

When we accept the myth that the best we can do is to simply "grin and bear it," we miss out on what mothering can mean. While we're wishing ourselves into the next season, we miss the good stuff that's happening now. This myth is shattered when we deliberately determine to make the most of life's irretrievable moments.

I often become overly concerned with the details of everyday life and forget my place in the big picture.

- *Live in the present.* How quickly we push past today to reach tomorrow!
  First I was dying to finish high school and start college.
  And then I was dying to finish college and start working.
  And then I was dying to marry and have children.
  And then I was dying for my children to grow old enough
  for school so I could return to work.
  And then I was dying to retire.
  And now, I am dying ...
  And suddenly I realize I forgot to live.
  —*Anonymous*

- Today you are indispensably valuable in the life of someone else!
  A hundred years from now ... it will not matter what my bank account was,
  the sort of house I lived in, or the kind of car I drove ...
  but the world may be different because I was important in the life of a child.
  —*Anonymous*

- This week you have the opportunity to get on the floor and build block towers. This is the season when you are invited to read, to play, to imagine, to dream! Your lap is the "favorite-est place to be." Your smile is more valuable than money. Your words mean more than those on the television, in a magazine, or in a classroom. Savor the moments of this season that will never come around again.
  Yesterday is history.
  Tomorrow is a mystery.
  Today is a gift.
  That's why we call it "The Present."
  —*Anonymous*

We tend to believe that life will get better when, really, it just gets different. If the grass looks greener on the other side of your fence, it may be because you're not investing time and energy in your own grass. Live in the present.

✿ Where do you tend to live mentally? Check one.

☐ In the past   ☐ In the present   ☐ In the future

How does perspective help us to combine the three time periods in a healthy way?

_____

- *Enjoy the little things.* Treasure each moment. Like precious stones, they are yours to touch, appreciate, and store in your heart to ponder and relive.
  For life is short, the years rush past.
  A little boy grows up so fast.
  No longer is he at your side,
  His precious secrets to confide.
  The picture books are put away.
  There are no more games to play.
  No goodnight kiss, no prayers to hear—
  That all belongs to yesteryear.
  My hands once busy now lie still.
  The days are long and hard to fill.
  I wish I might go back and do
  The little things you asked me to.
      —Anonymous

One last mothering myth tends to rob us of our mothering perspective.

Myth #4
Mothering is serious business and
at every moment the lives of your children are at stake.

Reality: Lighten up. Children are resilient. Handle them with honesty and humor. Fear obscures perspective. Focusing on the worst case scenario, the unimaginable horror of what even remotely might lie ahead, our fears leap out of all proportion and blur our vision of reality.

And our fears multiply. "Be sure to scrub your cutting board in hot soapy water every time you use it, or you could infect your entire family with the bacteria in the raw chicken you cut up." While good mothering is crucial, falling victim to the fear of ruining our children with a single mistake is unrealistic. Fight off this myth by recognizing that children are resilient.

If I don't read enough to my young children, I've heard that they'll never be admitted to the college of their choice. And what about fevers? If I don't take care of my baby's high fever, I just learned that her permanent teeth could come in permanently yellowed!

- *Honor your children with honesty.* When you make a mistake, learn to forgive yourself and let go of your failure. Refuse to pack up your guilt and carry it with you. Say you're sorry and move on. When your children ask questions, tell them the truth. Children do not expect their mothers to be perfect—unless we have taught them to expect perfection. They will respond with respect when inadequacies are shared appropriately.

In the same way, be forgiving of your children. Children most often respond to a light touch, not a heavy hand. Make "OOPS!" the password of your home. Take mothering just a little bit less seriously and watch your children blossom!

Four myths of mothering. If we believe them and what they stand for, we're sure to lose our focus. But when we replace them with reality, perspective returns.

♣ Determine some of your own mothering myths and realities. What are some of the "ditties" about mothering that echo in your mind like a broken record? (Example: "If it's worth doing, it's worth doing well.")

_____

_____

_____

Circle the ones you listed that are valuable to keep. Use the margin to rewrite the myths into realities.

A Perspective of Choice

One of the most challenging aspects of mothering is the challenge of choices. How do I know if I can/should go through delivery without medication? Should I go back to work after the baby is born? What philosophy of discipline will work best for my child? How do I choose a school or day-care program? And what about me? How and when should I take time for myself? What really matters in the long run?

Various descriptions have been used to explain the choice-making dilemma faced by mothers.

What Are Your Priorities?

Perspective for choice-making begins with identifying your priorities. But the process may not be as clear or simple as it sounds. If your priority is to stay home from work to attend to your child's nurturing needs, you have a clear priority. Simple choice. Right? Maybe ... except when you also need to work in order to put food on the table. Few children are happy and well-adjusted when they aren't fed.

Your husband may also be a priority. He wants you to spend more time alone with him. But your baby is sick and crying for you. What are you supposed to do? Which one gets top priority? Whose need do you put first?

You may recognize a priority for giving yourself a break and an opportunity for growth now and then, but what do you do when your toddler comes down with a cold the night of your first seminar?

I have to remember that I am a home-maker, not a house-keeper.

There are times when an assignment of priorities is both easy and helpful. But there are many other moments when the picture is not so clear, and the pieces keep shifting like the pattern in a kaleidoscope, which changes as you slowly rotate it in the light. There is no single clear priority all the time, or rigid, predetermined first-, second-, and third-place priority rankings which lead to the right choices.

What Is This Balancing Act?

Another view of perspective for choice-making is the balancing act. Choices are made on the basis of how good we are at juggling.

Like a circus act, a mom takes one plate and spins it on a stick above her head. Then another plate is added, so she must spin both plates. A bit later, here comes another and then another until she is spinning four and then five plates above her head. As if this were not enough, some new responsibility hits her around one leg. Now she must stand with all her weight on only one foot. Looking down, she realizes that her once-secure footing has been replaced by a thin wire, suspended high above the ground. With perspiration beading her brow, she fights for balance while keeping all the plates in motion. Because, of course, she must.

"For I know the plans I have for you, declares the LORD, plans to prosper you and not to harm you, plans to give you hope and a future."
Jeremiah 29:11

Life can't be kept neatly in balance. As soon as you decide that every child will participate in only one "outside" activity, your progeny are selected for children's chorale and make it to the finals of the state swim meet. We need something more than a balancing act to direct our perspective regarding choice-making.

♣ Read *This Week's Verse* on page 93. Which of these is the best way to achieve our mothering priorities?
- ☐ Seek first a clean, well-ordered house.
- ☐ Seek first attractive, well-mannered children.
- ☐ Seek first a good standard of living.
- ☐ Seek first getting your children into a good college.
- ☐ Seek first God and His activity in the world around you.

Seasoned Perspective

"There is a time
for everything,
and a season for
every activity
under heaven:
a time to be born
and a time to die,
a time to plant
and a time to uproot,
a time to kill
and a time to heal,
a time to tear down
and a time to build,
a time to weep
and a time to laugh,
a time to mourn
and a time to dance,
a time to scatter
stones and a time
to gather them,
a time to embrace
and a time to refrain,
a time to search
and a time to give up,
a time to keep and
a time to throw away,
a time to tear
and a time to mend,
a time to be silent
and a time to speak,
a time to love
and a time to hate,
a time for war
and a time for peace."

Ecclesiastes 3:1-8

Perhaps the most sensible approach to choice-making is the seasonal perspective. In this view, life is separated into various seasons, each characterized by its own priorities and its own criteria for choice-making. Looking at the *whole* of life with all its seasons enables us to gain perspective within each season. As one mother of a preschooler put it:

I love autumn. It is my favorite time of year, but I felt frustrated that it is such a brief season until I realized that its beauty is so poignant because it is framed by summer and winter. As a mother of a preschooler, I have to remind myself that each stage of life has its immense wonder, yet they all must move on. It is only in the moving on that we can fully appreciate what has passed.

In her book, *A Season at Home*, Debbie Barr writes about making choices with this seasonal perspective, which she describes as "sequencing," a process that allows women to concentrate on each of life's major tasks at the proper time.

Sequencing allows us to say "I love you" to our children in the most convincing way possible: by being there during the season of their lives when they need the most nurture and physical care. As the seasons of life unfold, we expand into other pursuits gradually, according to the guidance of God.[2]

The Bible describes this seasonal perspective in the Book of Ecclesiastes. Read the verses in the margin.

A time to mother tiny children and a time to mother older ones. A time to hold babies and a time to let them go. A time to focus on our children and a time to give attention to ourselves and our dreams.

An understanding of the whole of life helps us pay closer attention to where we are. We see the importance of choosing to invest in our children now—the season of their greatest need for us—knowing that other seasons will come later. "Not now, maybe later" reminds us that we are not sacrificing ourselves forever and that investment of time in our children now will pay dividends later as they become more independent, allowing us freedom to pursue other interests.

❀ Reread the *Mothering Maxim* on page 93. Put an X on the seesaw to describe how well you fit today into the bigger picture of life.

not very well　　　　　　　　　*fairly well*　　　　　　　　　*very well*

Mother-poet Joy Jacobs expresses her own commitment to sequencing in her "Mysteries of Motherhood":

Yesterday I found a fingernail in the toaster,
Today the dryer yields just seven socks.
Ah, mysteries of life:
Whence fingernails?
Where socks?
Where are the mates?
And why not six or eight?
I long to search for Holy Grails
Or even joust at windmills. ...
Instead, I rewash glasses
Left less than spot-free
By eager childish hands
And hang sheets out on windy days
And never do catch sight
of one brave armored knight.
But when a little boy thanks God at night
For "the best mommy in the world"—
Strange windmills lose their charm
And I'm content
To fetch a grail of water
Before he goes to sleep.
Quixote, wait another year!
I still am needed here.[3]

Keeping Things in Perspective

Perspective is the ability to stand between yesterday and tomorrow and understand how today fits and what matters most. How very much moms of preschoolers need perspective! We need to know that we're making a difference when we put a bit of ourselves on the shelf for a while. We need to know that when we drop everything to hold our babies while they are sick, or disregard the clutter to read to our toddlers, or just be present as a "home base" from which our little ones can go out to explore—we need to know that we've chosen well.

Max Lucado captures our need for perspective as he writes about a group of climbers scaling a tall mountain while keeping their snow-capped goal in sight: "As long as we can see our dream, as long as our goal is within eyesight, there is no mountain we can't climb or summit we can't scale. But take away our vision, block our view of the trail's end, and the result is as discouraging as the journey."[4]

Reality showed me I cannot be Supermom. The important thing is to leave a legacy and lead my children to God. The dishes can wait.

♣ Make your own stress sack with tangible reminders to let go of what's unimportant. Include items such as the ones you read below and others you find meaningful. Bring your stress sack to your next group meeting.

- A piece of chalk to use when something unpleasant happens, so you can "chalk it up" to experience.
- A tissue to remind you to dry someone's tears with a kind word, a note, or a hug.
- An eraser to remind you to wipe your slate clean.
- A thumbtack to remind you not to just sit on your problems. A-tack them one by one.
- A favorite cartoon, bumper sticker, or greeting card to remind you to laugh—often.
- A small stone to remind you God is your rock.
- A nail to remind you that Jesus coped with some pretty heavy stress, too.[5]

In the daily grind of mothering little-bitty ones, moms need to remember the bigger picture. Make the most of life's irretrievable moments. Every day is priceless and will never return. Decide now that you won't waste a single one.

Eternal Perspective

"Remember your Creator in the days of your youth." Ecclesiastes 12:1

Keeping the main thing the main thing requires us to remember our Creator, who alone defines our purpose in life and gives meaning to every day. When you are tempted to think that material things are the substance of life, remember Jesus' counsel to place your treasure—that is, your primary investment of time, talent, and resources—where dust, and moths, and rust cannot steal them away. Instead, place your treasure in heaven; invest in eternal things that will not pass away.

"Where your treasure is, there your heart will be also." Matthew 6:21

🌿 In the margin, read Matthew 6:21. Why did Jesus say the location of our treasure— that is, earth or heaven—is so important?

_____

Consider creating a wall hanging or other artistic reminder from the words below.

A New Day

This is the beginning of a new day. God has given me this day to use as I will. I can waste it—or use it for good, but what I do today is important, because I am exchanging a day of my life for it! When tomorrow comes, this day will be gone forever, leaving in its place something that I have traded for it. I want it to be gain, and not loss; good, and not evil; success, and not failure; in order that I shall not regret the price that I have paid for it.[6]

Hope

Sometimes I Wonder if There Is More to Life

This Week's Scripture
"Put your hope in God, for I will yet praise him, my Savior and my God."
Psalm 42:5

Mothering Maxim
Hope is a personal relationship with God, who meets all our needs.

She drew back the sliding door to the patio and closed it behind her. *Just a few minutes alone,* she thought. *I need a breather.* No good. Here came Samuel and Elizabeth to the door, smashing their faces up against the glass, their hot breath creating circles of steam on its surface. *"Mommy!* Come back in here!" Samuel hollered. Elizabeth raised her blanket, her face puckering in whimpers.

Carla opened the door a few inches. "Samuel and Elizabeth ... Mommy needs some quiet time. Go back to your movie, OK?"

She reached in her hand, and pulled the drapes shut. Maybe if they couldn't see her they would leave her alone. She shut the door again, held it closed, and sank down with her back against it, hugging her knees.

Now they came at her from beneath the curtains, pushing the drapes up in uneven lumps with their heads. "MOMMY!"

"Samuel and Elizabeth ... LEAVE ME ALONE!" Carla shouted. Both children stared wide-eyed at their usually composed mother. Elizabeth's whimpers turned to wails. Samuel put a protective arm about his baby sister as he led her out from underneath the drapes.

Carla let out a long and loud sigh. She stared back at her own reflection from the flat surface of the patio door. Creases in her brow. Bags under her eyes. Hair slicked back in a quick ponytail. Sweats that couldn't hide the presence of 15 stubborn, ever-present pounds.

She looked out at the small yard littered with big wheels and sandbox toys. Raising her eyes to the sky, she saw gray. Gray, gray, gray. Sky. Patio. Her mood.

It was only three o-clock in the afternoon, but she'd been up since five a.m. She'd already been to the store and the park. She'd made lunch. Then she'd read to the kids and put them down for naps. But they wouldn't sleep. They'd come at her with puzzles, books, books, and then whines to put a movie in the VCR. It was too much.

"I can't do this," Carla spat out the words. *I'm tired. I've got nothing left,* she thought to herself. *I didn't think mothering would be like this! I thought they'd sleep at some point during their lifetimes—and that I could do some things I wanted to do. I never dreamed I'd be losing it like this with my kids, wanting them to just leave me alone.*

Her silent monologue ceased. She simply sat, staring blankly ahead.

And then she felt a *clunk* against her back through the glass. Samuel was hurling Legos® at the curtains, trying to get her attention. Carla's head pounded. *I really can't do this,* she repeated to herself. *I can't go back in there.* Lifting her eyes heavenward, she asked aloud, "Is there any hope for me?"

Hopeless Situations

Have you ever felt like this mother? Your situation may have been different. Your husband just lost his job, and you're not sure how you'll pay the bills. Your mother has cancer and needs you, but you have three little ones who also need you. You're pregnant again and wonder in your heart if you can really afford ... love ... or cope with another child. Your marriage is stale. Your best friend is moving far away, and you don't know how you'll make it without her. Your neighborhood is full of crime—it's not safe to walk to the park anymore. Your house is a mess. Not only is there junk everywhere, but the paint is peeling, the bathtub drain is clogged, and the carpet is covered with stains. One of your children has been diagnosed with a disorder you don't understand, and the other one seems uncontrollable.

You feel like you can't do it anymore. It's too much. Life isn't turning out the way you expected, and there's not enough of you left to handle it.

> "Our problem is not so much that God doesn't give us what we hope for as it is that we don't know the right thing for which to hope. ... Hope is not what you expect."
> Max Lucado,
> *God Came Near*

🌸 Circle the words which characterize your mood most of the time. If none of these represents you, in the margin list other words that describe your prevalent mood.

discouraged	*patient*	*controlling*	*gentle*
accepting	*depressed*	*affirming*	*anxious*
angry	*affectionate*	*weak*	*responsible*
forgiving	*stressed*	*neglectful*	*content*

Misplaced Hope

You look for hope anywhere you think you might find it. If you could only change your **circumstances,** even for just a little while. *A vacation! That's what I need!* you think. So you make a plan, pack up husband and kids and two bags full of toys to keep them entertained in a cramped car, drive all night and half the next day, and check into a hotel already exhausted. The room doesn't have that lovely mountain view promised in the brochure. It looks out over the parking lot. The kids are raring to go, and you want to sleep. It rains for three days. Your youngest gets sick. And the sun comes out the day you leave.

Then you try **optimism.** You read an article in a magazine about how positive thinking can help you to be happier and healthier. The pessimist's feelings of helplessness and hopelessness damage the body's natural immune system, so the writer says. On the other hand, optimism protects one against illness. You wake in the morning, telling yourself you'll look on the bright side, but by nine o'clock you've been forced to deal with the dog mess on the carpet, spoiled milk in the refrigerator, and a dead battery in your car. *What* bright side?

Ah. **People.** Surely you can count on another person to give you hope—maybe your husband. Between errands and during precious nap time, you squeeze in a trial run on a new recipe, set a romantic table, and put the kids to bed early so you can be alone with him. But he wants to watch the game on TV. Or, you call up your best friend, arrange for a baby-sitter, and set a lunch date. But she gets the flu. And you end up taking her kids as well as yours so she can sleep.

OK. One last try—**self-help.** You hear on a talk show that if you look for goodness inside yourself, you'll find the confidence and comfort and strength your heart desires. But all you see is one mistake after another. Inadequacies. Failures. Fears. Insecurities. *What* goodness?

This is the worst yet. There's no way to take care of this feeling of emptiness and no option left to cover it up. You suddenly know you have nothing left. You can't do this for yourself, and you wonder if there is any reason left to hope.

♣ From the sources listed as misplaced hope, rank the order in which you turn to them for help, with 1 being your first choice and 4 your last.

☐ circumstances   ☐ optimism
☐ people   ☐ self-help

High Hopes

This is the toughest stuff of life. It's the place we all come to eventually. It hurts. It's called "reaching the end of ourselves."

Many people seek to fill that God-shaped emptiness with pleasure, prosperity, or power—anything but God, and yet the emptiness remains. Why? Because temporal things can never fill our emptiness.

The search for fulfillment in life must begin with God. Blaise Pascal said, "Man searches in vain, but finds nothing to help him, other than to see an infinite

"For I am convinced that neither death nor life, neither angels nor demons, neither the present nor the future, nor any powers, neither height nor depth, nor anything else in all creation, will be able to separate us from the love of God that is in Christ Jesus our Lord."
Romans 8:38-39

emptiness that can only be filled by One who is infinite and unchanging. In other words, it can only be filled by God Himself."[2]

Did you know that there is a God who is looking for you?

There is Someone who understands. He knows that what you want and need won't be found in a vacation, in positive thinking, in people, or in an attempt to reach down within yourself. He knows that you can't give yourself what you need. He knows you're tired. He knows you're empty. He knows there's nothing left.

How does He know? He knows because He is God. And He understands because He Himself lived what you are living. He sent His Son Jesus to walk the earth. He ate and slept ... and *didn't* sleep. He endured poverty, sickness, rejection, beatings, misjudgment, and pain. He knows your struggles.

And He wants to help you by being in a close relationship with you. You see, hope comes in a relationship. It is through a relationship with Jesus that your needs can be met completely and permanently.

As long as you believe you can take care of everything yourself and that you have all the goodness inside you to meet all your needs, you won't be able to receive the help Jesus has to offer. It's like this. A little boy was struggling to move a wagon, loaded with his prized possessions. His father watched his struggle from the front porch. Sweating and puffing, the boy hollered at his dad, "I can't budge this thing!"

"Have you tried everything you can try?"

"Yes!" sighed the tired boy.

"No, you haven't," called the father. "You haven't asked me for help."

In the Gospel of Matthew, Jesus spoke comforting words to every mother of preschoolers: "Come to me, all you who are weary and burdened, and I will give you rest" (Matt. 11:28). Jesus spoke these words to you. When you figure out that you can't meet all your needs, that there's a big empty hole in your heart that nothing else seems to fill—then you can turn to Jesus and ask for help.

You may be saying, "I have been a Christian for years. Of course, I know I can turn to Jesus for help!" But are you doing so? Having His power available to you does not necessarily mean you are using it. Let him be your source of help.

♣ Consider keeping a prayer journal where you record your prayer requests. Leave room to write the date the prayer is answered. Keep the journal for one month before you discard the idea. You'll be surprised at the encouragement and trust that will come from recording answers to prayers.

What if you have not yet become a Christian? On page 29 of this resource, you were given the opportunity to begin a relationship with Jesus that provides you with the hope your heart desires. Perhaps at that time you were not ready to take that step. Good news!

After I became a parent, it was easier for me to grasp the concept of God's love. As I went through all the triumphs and traumas of parenting and found myself still constantly loving my son, only then did I begin to understand God's ability to love me unconditionally.

God loves you. Do you want to know God's love? That's the path that leads you to Jesus.

Remember when you looked down into your heart to find the "goodness" within you and, instead, you found all those bad places? There's a word for this condition. The Bible calls it *sin*. Sin separates us from God because He is holy and perfect and can't dwell in the presence of sin. Where does that leave us? We're separated from the very Source who can provide help for us.

"For all have sinned and fall short of the glory of God." Romans 3:23

God chose to take care of this sin problem Himself by allowing His Son, Jesus, to die on the cross. His death pays for your sins and makes it possible for you to be forgiven for all the sinful spots—once and for all. Even when you don't deserve it. That's called *grace*. You've heard the old hymn, "Amazing Grace." Well, God's forgiveness is amazing. We don't deserve it. But we have it if we want it.

Do you want it? You can begin a relationship of hope with Him. All you have to do is ask.

🌼 If you do not have a relationship with Jesus as your Lord and Savior, pray this simple prayer:

Dear Jesus, I'm empty. When I look inside myself, I see soiled places that I now know are sin. Because of that sin, I know I cannot have a relationship with You. I need Your help. I believe that You died on the cross for me and for my sins. Please forgive me for my sins. I want to trust You as my Savior, and I want to know You as my Lord. Please come into my life and begin a relationship with me. Amen.

"Yet to all who received him, to those who believed in his name, he gave the right to become children of God." John 1:12

If you prayed that prayer just now as you read it, you can be sure that today you have a new reason for hope! How can we know that Jesus lives in us through His Spirit? Read the Scriptures in the margin. Underline the words that offer assurance of salvation.

You may not feel so different immediately, but you can start living with the promise that Jesus loves you and that He will help you day-by-day. You no longer have to live this life alone or dependent only upon yourself and your abilities. In fact, life was designed to be lived in partnership with Jesus, leaning on Him through everything that comes, drawing from His strength, depending upon His wisdom.

"He who has the Son has life; he who does not have the Son of God does not have life." 1 John 5:12

You may still have questions. That's OK. There are people who can help you find answers—counselors, pastors, church staff members, friends. There are books that will help you make sense of this personal relationship with Jesus. Or, simply start reading the Bible, say, in the Gospel of John or Mark. You probably won't understand it all. Don't worry. You don't have to. You don't have to understand electricity to use it, do you? You just have to plug something in or turn on a switch. A relationship with Jesus begins when you give what you know about yourself and your needs to what you know about Him.

Stumbling Blocks to Faith

Many times we run into obstacles or barriers that keep us from embracing faith in God. Here are a few of the barriers we erect between ourselves and God.

The Emotional Barrier—a set of negative feelings based on bad experiences with believers or with organized religion. We are confronted by the emotional barrier when we reject Christ because we have felt put down or pressured. It may seem that all believers in Christ are pushy and hypocritical.

The Intellectual Barrier—a tendency to disregard or reject Christ based upon bad information or misconceptions. We face an intellectual barrier, for instance, when we reject Christ because we assume the Bible is full of mistakes, or because we just cannot understand how a loving God could allow suffering in the world.

The Volitional Barrier—a natural inclination to resist examining spiritual things, or to reject Christ outright based upon independence, pride, or stubbornness. The Bible says this independence is rooted in our sinful nature. We encounter a volitional barrier when we refuse to examine the evidence for Christianity because we are afraid of what we might have to give up.[3]

Just as there are barriers that keep us from God, faith is the substance that leads us to God. Here are some descriptions of faith. Faith is ...

... not a leap in the dark nor a mystical experience nor an indefinable encounter with someone—but trust in One who has explained himself in a Person—Christ, in an historical record—the Bible ... remembering that in the kingdom of God everything is based on promise not on feeling.

... confidence in God's faithfulness to me in an uncertain world, on an uncharted course, through an unknown future.

... reliance on the certainty that God has a pattern for my life when everything seems meaningless.

... thanking God for his gift of emotional health, not assuming it all stems from my ability to cope with life.

... not a vague hope of a happy hereafter, but an assurance of heaven based on my trust in Christ's death as payment for my sins.

... refusing to feel guilty over past confessed sins, when God, the sovereign Judge, has declared me—"PARDONED!"

... realizing that God is the God of now, carrying on his purposes in every tedious, dull, stupid, boring, empty minute of my life.

... ceasing to worry, leaving the future to the God who controls the future.[4]

Hope for All Our Needs

When we look back through this book, chapter by chapter, and revisit each need in the light of a relationship with Jesus, we can see that He can be like sunbeams shining through the clouds on a gray day. Let's look at some of the things we've learned, one by one.

"My God will meet all your needs according to his glorious riches in Christ Jesus." Philippians 4:19

Significance: Sometimes I Wonder if Mothering Matters.
Mothering *does* matter. Add to the truth of this chapter that all our "doing" will never be enough to earn us the kind of consistent significance in life that we long for; that God alone provides the ultimate meaning for our lives. Suddenly, our doing doesn't define us or confine us! All at once we're free to be the best mothers we can be because our ultimate worth is not dependent upon our role of mothering.

Identity: Sometimes I'm Not Sure Who I Am.
God made each one of us, and we are precious in His sight. When we learn to see ourselves as God sees us—forgiven and free from sin—we are truly free to drop our burdens of guilt over not being good enough and become all He created us to be.

Growth: Sometimes I Long to Develop Who I Am.
God has placed unique potential within each of us. That potential can be fully developed and completely fulfilled only through a relationship with Him. We find that change and growth are possible as His power changes us.

Intimacy: Sometimes I Long to Be Understood.
As much as we'd like to, we can't always count on other people. Eventually, they will disappoint us. Nobody's perfect. They'll hurt our feelings or let us down. Only God is perfect. And only His love for us is pure and unconditional. In a relationship with Jesus, we can find the intimacy and understanding we need. He knows us the best and loves us the most.

Instruction: Sometimes I Don't Know What to Do.
The Bible contains many practical principles and truths that tell us how to live. There is also truth in the world that can provide us with direction, because all real truth is God's truth. Ultimately, the truth is found in a person. Read John 14:6 in the margin. This truth helps us make good choices.

"Jesus answered, 'I am the way and the truth and the life. No one comes to the Father except through me.'" John 14:6

Help: Sometimes I Need to Share the Load.
We weren't meant to mother alone. When we admit our need for help, God can meet it. He wants us to learn to trust Him to be in control of the uncontrollable part

of our lives. He wants us to value ourselves enough to seek help from those He has placed in our lives to offer such help—husbands, children, extended family, friends, and the church family.

Recreation: Sometimes I Need a Break.

Recreation is really re-creation. God created us with the need to rest. He also makes us new creatures when we come into a relationship with Jesus. Each day is a new beginning when we begin it with Him. And He refreshes and renews us on an on-going basis as we seek Him.

Perspective: Sometimes I Lose My Focus.

I see now that my real need has always been for God. Motherhood is too hard to go it alone.

Perspective means developing a God-view of life. When we learn to see life as He does, to value what He values, to evaluate decisions and daily matters in terms of what matters in eternity, we obtain a whole new perspective.

Real hope is finding the Source who meets all needs.

✿ Of the needs we have reviewed during this study, rate the degree to which you feel you are addressing each of them, with 1= not addressing it at all and 5= on top of this one! Then go back and think of the ways to address some of your 1's and 2's.

- ☐ significance
- ☐ identity
- ☐ growth
- ☐ intimacy
- ☐ instruction
- ☐ help
- ☐ recreation
- ☐ perspective
- ☐ hope

A Relationship of Hope

You have made us for yourself, O God, and our hearts are restless till they find rest in you.
Augustine's
Confessions

Beginning a relationship with Jesus will not mean that all your problems will fade away. You won't find yourself suddenly perfect in all your interactions. Nope. Beginning a relationship with Jesus is just that: *a beginning.* It will take time for Him to change you. You will gradually learn to trust Him with more and more areas of your world as you get to know Him better.

As in all relationships, your relationship with Jesus will grow and develop as you work at it. As you invest yourself, you'll reap dividends. As you learn, you'll grow. Remember, this relationship with Jesus allows you to have a relationship with the God of the universe! Because Jesus died for our sins and God raised Him from the dead, Jesus is alive and stands ready to be active in your life!

Two practices will be vital to growing in your relationship with Jesus.

Talking

As in all relationships, communication is essential to knowing. In order to get to know God better, we have to talk to Him.

Talking with God doesn't have to be complicated or even very formal. Prayer is merely having a conversation with God. It's telling Him what's on your mind and in your heart. In his book, *Prayer*, Richard Foster describes how to talk to God: "Simple Prayer involves ordinary people bringing ordinary concerns to a loving and compassionate Father."[5]

Foster offers a sample of this kind of regular talking to God: "Sometimes Simple Prayer is called the 'Prayer of Beginning Again,'" Foster writes. "We make mistakes, we sin, we fall down, but each time we get up and begin again. We pray again. We seek to follow God again. And again we are defeated. Never mind. We confess and begin again ... and again ... and again."[6]

Set aside a time to talk to God each day. Maybe when you first open your eyes in the morning before you even throw back the covers. Maybe as you rock your little ones to sleep at nap time or bedtime. Maybe the first few minutes of their nap time. But keep looking until you find a regular time to meet with God.

Talk to Him about the day-to-day business of your life. God is always present and available. We don't have to make an appointment to get His attention.

❀ Check the following times you could talk to Jesus during the day:

☐ As you wash dishes   ☐ As you shower   ☐ As you run the vacuum
☐ As you drive alone   ☐ As you fold laundry ☐ As you walk (exercise)

☐ Other? _____

When you're wondering how to handle your child's tantrum, ask Jesus. If you're not sure if you should be working outside the home during these years, talk it over with Him. You don't have to keep all your questions inside. When you're in a relationship with Jesus, He is ready and willing to hear and help.

Listening

As important as it is to talk to God, it is equally vital to listen to what He says. No, He doesn't usually communicate with folks through an audible voice. But He does get His thoughts across through His Holy Spirit.

When you pray, pause long enough to "listen." God may want to tell you something in response to your prayer. Sometimes we simply don't have what we need because we're never still enough to listen to what God is trying to get across to us. But as we practice listening, we'll learn how to hear His whispers more and more often.

He'll speak to you when you're reading the Bible (His Word). Find a translation of the Bible that is easy to read and understand. Some paraphrases are also helpful as we first begin to read God's Word—Eugene Peterson's *The Message*, for example. Start out with the Psalms or a Gospel (Matthew, Mark, Luke, or John) or a small New Testament book, like 1 John or Ephesians, and go on from there. Because the Bible is God's Word, it is the major tool available to us for getting to know Him. Don't neglect it.

♣ Here are some ideas for enhancing your Bible study time. Check those which you already practice. Star those you want to act on in the near future.

- ☐ Ask for a new translation of the Bible as a holiday or birthday gift.
- ☐ Mark key passages; underline verses; write key ideas in the margin of your Bible.
- ☐ As you read, have handy a good Bible dictionary and Bible concordance.
- ☐ Commit key verses to memory.
- ☐ Place copies of Bible verses you want to remember in high traffic areas of your home, such as bathroom mirrors, over the kitchen sink, on the refrigerator, etc.
- ☐ Read the Bible through in a year. A plan for doing so is found in *Open Windows*, a daily devotional guide available from LifeWay Christian Resources. Order by calling 1-800-458-2772.

"Hope deferred makes the heart sick, but a longing fulfilled is a tree of life."
Proverbs 13:12

Sometimes God will speak through your relationships with other people who are Christians. When we share our concerns and questions with those who have been in a relationship with God longer, we find strength and help. God will use His people to help you. And before you know it, He'll use you to help others! This is what the church is all about. Visit a church in your area. Find out about their beliefs and whether or not they match up with what you read in the Bible. Attend services and consider becoming a member.

"They devoted themselves to the apostles' teaching and to the fellowship, to the breaking of bread and to prayer. Every day they continued to meet together in the temple courts. They broke bread in their homes and ate together with glad and sincere hearts."

But you will soon learn that "church" means much more than a building. God intended His people to be in fellowship together, to study the Bible together, to worship together, to learn to depend upon one another, and to reach out to others— together. This is called "community" and within this kind of loving and sharing atmosphere, many of us find the sense of family we might not have had in our own nuclear families. In community, we focus and grow in our relationships with God and with other people.

🌿 In the margin, read a description of the church in Jerusalem in Acts 2:42,46. List reasons for the sense of community felt by these early believers:

_____

We hope you listed the teaching ministry of the church, praise, and prayer, along with fellowship at mealtimes. The Bible teaches us that we must be in intentional Christian community in order to become the people God intends us to be. So find a church home. Join a Bible study—a group of folks who come together to study God's Word. Get involved in serving others and meeting their needs. Share with your husband and your children what you are learning about Jesus.

Your relationship with God is a relationship between living souls. It will grow and change and deepen as you invest yourself in it. You can expect to change and for your relationships with others to be different as well. Jesus loves us too much to leave us just the way we are. You may discover that you will have to apologize after making a mistake rather than ignoring your offense. You may need to grow in an attitude of patience or humility. You might even find that you have whole areas of your life that Jesus wants to touch and heal. He may want you to risk—to venture out into something you've never done before, to a place where you've never been. But even the desire for these changes comes from God. And He will help us through them. That's one of His promises.

❧ List growth areas you have identified through this study that you feel God's leading to develop in your life. If you do not have a growth plan, use the margin to list specific steps you are taking to make these changes.

_____

_____

Is there hope for you? You bet. Trust Him. Jesus knows what you need. And He can meet those needs better than you can meet them alone.

In the Book of Isaiah, the prophet described God's tender care for His nation of Israel. God's words in this Old Testament book—written some four thousand years ago—are for every mother of preschoolers today. Using a shepherd metaphor, the prophet encouraged His people with this loving description of God: "He tends his flock like a shepherd: He gathers the lambs in his arms and carries them close to his heart; he gently leads those that have young" (Isa. 40:11).

❧ Reread *This Week's Verse* and the *Mothering Maxim* on page 105. Summarize your reason for hope:

_____

End Notes

Chapter 1: Significance

1. Phyllis Diller in *A Mother Is to Cherish* (Nashville, TN: Thomas Nelson, 1994).
2. Anne Morrow Lindbergh, *Gift from the Sea* (New York: Pantheon, 1955), 46-47.
3. Jan Johnson, "Stay at Home Moms," *Virtue* (January/February, 1990): 32.
4. Joan France, "A 'Caretaker' Generation," *Newsweek* (January 29, 1990): 16.
5. Juanita Fletcher, "Rostrum," *U.S. News and World Report* (August 8, 1988): 8.
6. Jill Zook-Jones interview with Brenda Hunter, "The Maternal Imperative," *Christianity Today* (March 7, 1994): 15.
7. Katherine Butler Hathaway, *The Little Locksmith*, (New York: Coward- McCann, 1943), 21.
8. *Starting Points: The Report on the Carnegie Task Force on Meeting the Needs of Young Children* (New York: Carnegie Corporation of New York, April 1994).
9. Sandra Pipp in Mary McArthur, "Whose Baby Are You?" *Colorado Alumnus* (December 1993): 5.
10. Sigmund Freud, *Outline of Psychoanalysis SE 23* (London: Hogarth Press, 1940), 188.
11. Dr. Marianne Neifert in Betty Johnson, "The Juggling Act of Dr. Mom," *Virtue* (March/April 1994): 38.
12. Quoted in Bob Kelly's *Reflections* (1990).

Chapter 2: Identity

1. Gregg Lewis, "Good News About Me," *Campus Life* (October 1986): 31.
2. Erik Fromm, *The Art of Living* (New York: Harper & Row, 1956), 43.
3. B.J. Cohler and H.V. Grunebaum, *Mothers, Grandmothers, and Daughters* (New York: Wiley, 1981) in Brenda Hunter, *Home by Choice* (Portland, OR: Multnomah Press, 1993), 32.
4. John Trent, *Life Mapping* (Colorado Springs, CO: Focus on the Family; 1994), 81.
5. Martha Thatcher, "The Most Difficult Love," *Discipleship Journal 35* (1986): 19.
6. Cecil Osborne, *The Art of Learning to Love Yourself* (Grand Rapids, MI: Zondervan, 1976), 38.
7. Barbara Johnson, *Stick a Geranium in Your Hat and Be Happy* (Dallas, TX: Word, 1990), 107-8.
8. Valerie Bell, *Getting Out of Your Kids' Faces and Into Their Hearts* (Grand Rapids, MI: Zondervan, 1994), 73.
9. Ibid.
10. A.W. Tozier, *That Incredible Christian* (Harrisburg, PA: Christian Publications, 1964), 102-3. Used by permission.
11. Richard J. Foster, *Prayers from the Heart* (San Francisco: HarperSanFrancisco, 1994), 54.

Chapter 3: Growth

1. Susan Solomon Yem, "Heading Home," *Virtue* (January/February 1995): 44.
2. William J. Bennett, *The Book of Virtues* (New York: Simon & Schuster, 1993), 12.
3. Ted Engstrom, *The Pursuit of Excellence* (Grand Rapids, MI: Zondervan, 1982), 17.
4. Gary Hardaway, "When Dreams Die," *Moody Monthly* (June 1986): 20.
5. Barbara Sher with Annie Gottlieb, *Wishcraft* (New York: Ballantine Books, 1979), 5.
6. Dottie McDowell, "Dottie's Delight Article," in Dave Ray, *Mom's Check-Up* (Royal Oak, MI: Core Ministries, 1994), 11.
7. Hellen Ferris, ed., *Favorite Poems Old and New* (Garden City, NY: Doubleday, 1957), 22.
8. Brenda Hunter, *What Every Mother Needs to Know* (Sisters, OR: Multnomah Press, 1993) 59.

Chapter 4: Intimacy

1. John Townsend, *Hiding from Love* (Colorado Springs, CO: NavPress, 1991), 34.
2. Heidi Brennan in Brenda Hunter, *In the Company of Women* (Sisters, OR: Questar, 1994), 25.
3. Paul Tournier, *To Understand Each Other* (Atlanta, GA: John Knox Press, 1967), 29-30.
4. Brenda Hunter, *In the Company of Women* (Sisters, OR: Questar, 1994), 115-16.
5. Heidi Brennan in Brenda Hunter, *In the Company of Women* (Sisters, OR: Questar, 1994), 25.
6. Ibid., 26.
7. Joan Wulff, "Searching for Community in an Individualistic Age," *His Magazine* (March 1982): 1.
8. Richard Fowler, "The Intimacy Trap," *Discipleship Journal* 25 (1985): 12.
9. *Rocky Mountain News* (April 7, 1985).
10. Donna Partow, *No More Lone Ranger Moms* (Minneapolis, MN: Bethany House, 1995), 31.
11. Walter Wangerin, Jr., "You Are, You Are, You Are," *The Lutheran Journal* (January 24, 1990): 5.
12. Dale Hanson Bourke, *Everyday Miracles: What Motherhood Really Means* (Dallas TX: Word, 1989), 4.
13. Cecil Osborne, *The Art of Understanding Your Mate* (Grand Rapids, MI: Zondervan, 1970), 159-60.
14. Elizabeth Cody Newenhuyse, "Friendship Fizzle," *Today's Christian Woman* (January/February, 1995): 51.

Chapter 5: Instruction

1. William Sears, M.D. and Martha Sears, R.N., *The Baby Planner* (Nashville, TN: Thomas Nelson, 1994), 2.
2. Reprinted and adapted from Cindy Tolliver, *At-Home Motherhood*. (San Jose, CA: Resource Publications, Inc., 1994), 24-26.
3. Adapted material by Eric Swanson for Campus Crusade for Christ (unpublished).
4. Susan L. Lenzkes, *When the Handwriting on the Wall Is in Brown Crayon* (Grand Rapids: Zondervan, 1981), 18.
5. From *Learning to Learn* by Gloria Frender, © 1990 by Incentive Publications, Inc., Nashville, TN 37215. Used by permission.

Chapter 6: Help

1. Donna Partow, *No More Lone Ranger Moms* (Minneapolis, MN: Bethany House, 1995), 13.
2. Ruth Barton, *Becoming a Woman of Strength* (Wheaton, IL: Harold Shaw, 1994), 193, 205.
3. Patricia Sprinkle, *Do I Have to?* Grand Rapids, MI: Zondervan, 1993), 16.
4. Taken Patricia Sprinkle, *Do I Have To?* (Copyright 1993 by Patricia Sprinkle. Used by permission of Zondervan Publishing House), 106-7.
5. Ibid, 87
6. Adapted from Gwen Ellis, *Thriving As a Working Woman* (Wheaton, IL: Tyndale House Publishers, 1995), 42-50.
7. Susan Yates, "And Then I Had Kids!" *Focus on the Family* (May 1990): 4.

Chapter 7: Recreation

1. Dolores Curran, "Women and Fatigue," *Denver Catholic Register* (October 20, 1986).
2. Anne Morrow Lindbergh, *Gift from the Sea* (New York: Pantheon Books, 1955), 39.
3. Dr. Holly Atkinson in Dolores Curran, "Women and Fatigue," *Denver Catholic Register* (October 20, 1986).
4. Tim Hansel, *When I Relax, I Feel Guilty* (Elgin, IL: David C. Cook, 1979), 40.
5. Associated Press, "Study Finds Mother's Stress Affects Relations with Tots," *The Denver Post* (August 13, 1994).
6. Op. cit., Curran.
7. Denise Turner, "Keys to Happier Mothering," *Christian Herald* (May 1986), 23.
8. Grace Ketterman and Pat Holt, *When You Feel Like Screaming* (Wheaton, IL: Harold Shaw, 1988), 48.
9. William Arthur Ward, "Think It Over," *Fort Worth Star Telegram*.
10. Barbara Johnson, *Spatula Ministries Newsletter* (La Habra, CA: January, 1993).
11. H. Jackson Brown, Jr., *Life's Little Instruction Book* (Nashville, TN: Rutledge Hill Press, 1991).
12. Melanie McLean Michel, "Rock Around the Tot," *Aspire* (February/March 1995), 81.
13. Stacey C. York in Donna Partow, *No More Lone Ranger Moms* (Minneapolis, MN: Bethany House, 1995), 38.
14. Reprinted and adapted from Cindy Tolliver, *At-Home Motherhood* (San Jose, CA: Resource Publications, 1994), 178-80.
15. Gordon Dahl, *Work, Play, and Worship in a Leisure-Oriented Society* (Minneapolis, MN: Augsberg, 1972), 12.

Chapter 8: Perspective

1. Dr. Marianne Neifert in Betty Johnson, "The Juggling Act of Dr. Mom," *Virtue* (March/April 1994): 39
2. Debbie Barr, *A Season at Home* (Grand Rapids, MI: Zondervan. 1993), 26.
3. Joy Jacobs, "Mysteries of Motherhood," *Christian Herald* (May 1986), 22.
4. Max Lucado, *God Came Near* (Portland, OR: Multnomah, 1987), 160.
5. Adapted from Barbara Johnson, *Mama, Get the Hammer: There's a Fly on Papa's Head* (Dallas, TX: Word, 1994), 42.
6. Dr. Heartsill Wilson, "A New Day" (self-published).

Chapter 9: Hope

1. Mayo Mathers, "What My Children Have Taught Me," *Today's Christian Woman* (November/December 1994), 90.
2. Ibid.
3. "Heart for the Harvest" (1991). Used by permission of Search Ministries, 5038 Dorsey Hall Dr., Ellicott City, M.D. 21042.
4. Excerpted from Pamela Reeve, *Faith Is . . .* (Portland, OR: Multnomah Books, 1970).
5. Richard J. Foster, *Prayer: Finding the Heart's True Home* (Bloomington, MN: Garborg's, 1993), January 11.
6. Ibid., January 10.

A Special Letter to Mothers of Preschoolers

You have just completed a Bible study workbook that helps you identify your needs and address them. No doubt you have realized that understanding your own basic needs helps you become a better mom.

Would you like ongoing encouragement and support? That's what MOPS is all about.

MOPS stands for Mothers of Preschoolers, a program designed for mothers with children under school age. Women in MOPS come from different backgrounds and lifestyles, yet have similar needs and a shared desire to be the best mothers they can be.

As stated in the Introduction, a MOPS group is not a Bible study, but is based on instruction with biblical values that will continue to equip you for the responsibilities of family and community. A MOPS group provides a caring, accepting atmosphere for all mothers of preschoolers and gives moms the opportunity to share concerns and explore areas of creativity, in addition to the teaching.

The MOPS program also includes MOPPETS, a loving, learning experience for children. Approximately 2,200 MOPS groups currently meet in churches in the United States and 11 other countries to meet the needs of nearly 100,000 women.

MOPS also offers:

- Leadership training through resources, workshops, and mentoring. MOPS groups are primarily led by the mothers themselves, with the assistance of a MOPS Mentor.

- Connection to an international network of leaders through newsletters, a radio program, conventions, and a Web site.

- A dynamic, time-tested program that has proven effective in many adaptations, including suburban, urban, teen, rural, and international settings. When you start a MOPS group, you will receive all the materials you need to begin a successful MOPS program.

- The MOPS Shop, featuring books and quality products specifically designed for mothers of preschoolers.

- An outreach ministry, through the local church, to mothers of preschoolers. Specifically designed resources, available through MOPS, train moms in lifestyle evangelism.

To receive information, such as how to join a MOPS group, or how to receive other MOPS resources, such as *Mom Sense* newsletter, call or write MOPS International, P.O. Box 102200, Denver, CO 80250-2200, phone 1-800-929-1287, email: **Info@MOPS.org,** Web site: **http://www.MOPS.org.** To learn how to start a MOPS group, call 1-888-910-MOPS. For MOPS products, call The MOPS Shop at 1-888-545-4040.

Leader Guide for Bible Study Groups

This leader guide will help you facilitate ten group sessions—an introductory session and nine weekly Bible study sessions—of one hour in length. If you have more than one hour, you ask the discussion questions or add questions of your own. Feel free to adapt these suggestions to fit the needs of your group.

Distribute the books during the introductory session or at least one week in advance of session 1. Arrange the chairs in a semicircle and plan to sit as part of the group. Consult the *Before the Session* section of each lesson plan. Use the check-in sheet as a means of contacting absentees during the week. Consider using prayer partners as another avenue for contact and encouragement during the study.

Childcare will significantly affect attendance. If possible, provide childcare at the church. Consider enlisting senior adults or older teenagers to help with childcare, or help participants arrange homes where children from two or more families might combine resources to meet childcare needs.

Be aware of outreach possibilities with this study. You may want to invite mothers from your church or neighboring churches, your neighborhood, or your workplace. Leave advertisements in doctors' and dentists' offices, as well as childcare providers, day cares, and elementary schools near your church. Publicize the study through your women's enrichment ministry, the church newsletter, Bible study classes, and weekday ministries.

Introductory Session

Before the Session

1. Prepare a sign-in sheet for use each week. For this session and session 1, provide name tags and markers. Place these items near the door.
2. Have books available to distribute. If payment is expected, prepare a cash box to make change.
3. Post two large tear sheets on the focal wall of the room. Label one "Mothering Questions" and the other "Mothering Answers." Place a marker beneath each sheet.

During the Session

1. Upon arrival, direct participants to sign in and make name tags.
2. Ask them to go immediately to the tear sheets and to write at least one "question" they hope this study will address and then one "answer" or action that has helped them as mothers.

3. Begin the session by introducing yourself and telling about your family. If possible, share a humorous mothering incident to break the ice with any visitors. Then encourage participants to introduce themselves and tell about their families.
4. Read selected questions and answers from the tear sheets. Explain that you will keep these questions in mind as you proceed through the study.
5. Distribute the books and collect money if necessary. Discuss any housekeeping issues, such as childcare, meeting times and place (if different from this session).
6. Invite participants to turn to the Table of Contents and overview the nine mothering needs. Ask them to check the needs that seem most apparent to them at this stage in their

lives. Then, encourage volunteers to share the needs they checked.

7. Call for a volunteer to read aloud the opening case study on page 4. Ask: *Is this situation familiar to you? How would you have felt in the same situation?* Explain that case studies (real-life situations) and quotes from mothers are included throughout the book.

8. Ask participants to turn to Week 1 and scan pages 9-20. Call attention to the *Mothering Maxim* and *This Week's Verse*. If you choose to emphasize memorizing each week's Scripture verse, ask for the group's commitment. Review Proverbs 22:6 on page 9.

9. Explain that members should read the week's content and complete the learning activities prior to each group session. Emphasize the value of the Bible study questions and learning activities, which are practical suggestions for implementing the information they learn.

Closing the Session

1. If this session was for the purpose of introduction to help attendees decide whether or not to continue, explain how you want to receive their decision. Otherwise, announce the the next meeting time and assign the Introduction and Week 1 to be read by that time.

2. If your group is made up of persons who do not know one another well, you will want to use discretion in calling for prayer requests. List requests on your personal paper and pray for them during the coming week.

3. Close with a prayer for each mom and child represented. Thank God for the privilege of being mothers.

Session 1
Significance: Sometimes I Wonder if Mothering Matters

Before the Session

1. On the chalkboard, draw a seesaw similar to the one on the front cover of the workbook.

2. Have available name tags, sign-in sheet, and extra books if needed.

3. During the week, pray for each participant.

During the Session

1. Direct participants to sign in and prepare name tags, if needed.

2. Read or say together *This Week's Verse* (p. 9). Lead a prayer for God's blessings as you meet.

3. Call attention to the seesaw on the chalkboard. Ask moms to identify the two elements we are seeking to balance in Week 1 (need for significance/constant and often repetitive demands of motherhood). At each end of the

seesaw, record the group's response.

4. Ask volunteers to share how they responded to the first activity on page 11. Gauge from reactions the degree to which your group feels a need for personal significance. If it is a major concern, spend time carefully reviewing "The Difference That Mothering Makes" (pp. 16-20). Ask a volunteer to read aloud "You Are a Key Person" (p. 19).

5. Invite those who composed job descriptions to share them with the group.

6. Share and discuss results of the cost savings research activity suggested on page 16.

7. Remind moms that God designed the model for families. Assign each of the four biblical mothers listed on page 20 to a team of 2-3 persons. Using the verses listed beside the

assigned name, ask each team to answer the following questions:

1. Who was(were) her child(ren)?
2. Why might she have questioned her value?
3. What difference did her mothering make?

Be sensitive to moms who may not feel comfortable looking up Scriptures. Allow 3-5 minutes for discussion, then call for team reports. Invite moms to name other influential mothers. Say together *This Week's Verse* on page 9.

8. Invite volunteers to share their responses to the question at the bottom of page 20.

Closing the Session

1. Say together the *Mothering Maxim* on page 9.
2. Encourage participants to choose a prayer partner from the group. Ask partners to contact each other during the week to share concerns and praises and to support each other in their daily study. Make participation voluntary.
3. Pray, thanking God for the value He places on each person present.

Session 2

Identity: Sometimes I'm Not Sure Who I Am

Before the Session

1. Draw the seesaw on the chalkboard (see session 1).
2. Attach a large tear sheet to a focal wall. Provide markers.
3. Cut out three-inch diameter circles from brightly colored construction paper, making more circles than the number of moms anticipated. On each circle write a complimentary quality, such as friendly, sweet, kind, perky, curious, funny, happy, creative. Attach a straight pin to each circle and place circles near the entry door.

During the Session

1. As moms sign in, ask each one to choose a circle that represents one of her qualities and to wear it during the session.
2. Refer to the seesaw drawing. Ask, *What are we seeking to balance in this week's study?* (need for personal identity/roles as wife and mother). Write the answer on the seesaw.

3. Read aloud Mark 12:30-31. Ask, *Why is it important to love ourselves?* Then ask, *What is the difference between pride and self-worth?* After several responses, select one member to read a description of pride from Deuteronomy 8:11-19 and another to read descriptions of our worth in Psalm 139:14-16 and Matthew 6:25-26.
4. Explain that feeling good about ourselves is a testimony to our Creator's handiwork. He gives us value. When we refuse an honest compliment, we are denying the worth of our Creator's masterpiece!
5. Invite volunteers to explain why they chose their particular circles and/or how they responded to the second activity on page 22.
6. Allow those who designed business cards (p. 23) to reproduce them on the tear sheet attached to the focal wall. While they are drawing, encourage remaining moms to share activities that keep them from being consumed by the needs of their families. Then, have moms read their business cards.

7. Review the types of people we are *not* from pages 25-26. Ask, *Who are we meant to become like?* Discuss ways we can fully accept God's love for us from the truths on page 30. Ask volunteers to share which of these truths is especially important to them.

8. Repeat together the *Mothering Maxim* and *This Week's Verse* (p. 21). Discuss, *What is one "new" thing God is doing in your life right now?*

Closing the Session

1. Suggest that if anyone prayed to receive Christ as a result of this week's study, you (or a designated person) will be available to talk with her following the closing prayer. Do not ask for this information publicly.

2. With books open to page 32, ask moms to read together the prayer of acceptance. Close with a spoken prayer.

Session 3
Growth: Sometimes I Long to Develop Who I Am

Before the Session

1. Print the words, "My dream is..." on a strip of paper for each mom, leaving space for a short paragraph response. Place strips near the door alongside pens or pencils and a basket.

2. Ask someone to review the Book of Ruth, noting ways Naomi was a "nudger" to Ruth.

During the Session

1. As moms sign in, direct them to take one of the sentence strips, complete the sentence, and put it in the basket.

2. Read aloud each "My dream is..." statement, allowing moms to guess who wrote it. Some statements may appear humorous or outlandish, but approach them seriously unless told differently. Validate each person's dream.

3. Ask those who brought "dreamcatchers" to share them (p. 36). Summarize by saying that dreams motivate us to stretch beyond our skills, interests, and comfort zones.

4. Using the content in Week 3, brainstorm reasons we need to continue to grow, listing them on the chalkboard. Ask, *What are some "costs" of growth?* (p. 40).

6. Select someone to read aloud Colossians 1:9-13. Summarize Paul's dream for the Christians in Colossae: growth in the knowledge of God's will, a life pleasing to God, good works, and great endurance and patience. Apply these growth goals to mothering young children. Remind moms that Paul says these goals are realized through prayer.

7. Review the role of a nudger (p. 42). Ask moms to identify individuals who have been nudgers to them.

8. Call on the person enlisted to explain ways Naomi was a nudger to Ruth. Conclude her report by encouraging moms to be nudgers to one another.

9. Invite volunteers to share one or more of the growth goals they listed on pages 43-44.

Closing the Session

1. Form teams of 2-3 persons each and encourage them to pray specifically for one another's growth goals.

2. Reconvene the large group. Say together *This Week's Verse* and the *Mothering Maxim* on page 33. Close with a spoken prayer.

Session 4
Intimacy: Sometimes I long to Be Understood

Before the Session

1. If prayer partners were chosen earlier in the study, determine a plan for moms to change partners at the next session.

2. Write the following verses of Scripture on strips of paper for distribution during the session: Exodus 20:1-3; Psalm 62:5-8; Matthew 22:37-38; John 15:4-5.

During the Session

1. Ask, *Did you identify with the woman in the story on pages 45-46?* Then ask them to share their responses to the activity on page 46.

2. Say: *We need friendships. One reason is given in this week's Mothering Maxim.* Ask someone to read it aloud and state the reason.

3. Discuss the issue of loneliness, asking:
   - Why does loneliness appear to be on the increase?
   - Why is it hard to make and keep close friends?
   - What are some stumbling blocks to true intimacy?

4. Caution moms about seeking intimacy with their children. Discuss the activity on page 51. Point out that several of these actions would depend on the situation. Brainstorm general guidelines for conduct. Encourage moms to practice actions 3 and 7 on the list.

5. Invite moms to react to this statement from page 53. "Seeking intimacy in marriage alone puts too much strain on the relationship. ... Don't expect your husband to meet all your needs."

6. Ask someone to define and give an example of emotional adultery (p. 55).

7. Call for responses to the activity at the top of page 56. Add suggestions to the list.

8. Distribute the Scripture verses to four moms. After each passage has been read aloud, lead the group to summarize truths from the verses in two or three sentences. Ask a volunteer to record the truths on the chalkboard.

9. Repeat together *This Week's Verse* (p. 45). Say, *We find the truest and most satisfying intimacy in relationship with God.*

Closing the Session

1. *Optional:* Discuss a plan for changing prayer partners. Thank moms for their prayer support and encourage them to continue.

2. Invite moms to voice sentence prayers, thanking God for being our best Friend and most intimate Companion.

Session 5
Instruction: Sometimes I Don't Know What to Do

Before the Session

1. On a poster or tear sheet, write these words at random (mixed order): instincts, knowledge, values, experts.

2. Provide a display table for books (p. 63).

Bring some of your favorites and arrange them on the table. (Be sure to write your name prominently in the front of each.)

3. If possible, display some or all of the resources listed at the top of page 66.

4. Be prepared to tell about upcoming study opportunities in your church; distribute written information if possible.

During the Session

1. As moms sign in, collect their books and arrange them on the display table.

2. Say, *All of us face situations for which there are no clear answers.* Ask volunteers to share some of the situations or topics they listed in the activity on page 58. Do not discuss issues at this time; simply list on the chalkboard.

3. Ask two volunteers to read aloud the following Scriptures: Genesis 27:1-13 and Exodus 2:1-10. Discuss decisions made by these women and the consequences. Draw implications for moms as they make decisions for their children.

4. Emphasize the decision-making model on page 59. Apply it to a decision you have faced. Invite volunteers to share how they have used these steps to make decisions.

5. Display the poster prepared earlier. Ask moms to call out the order in which they tend to make decisions. For example, some lead with their hearts (values) but look for experts who agree with their opinions. Others depend on instincts, yet look for confirmation in books. Say, *There is value in using multiple sources of information without relying excessively on one.*

6. Refer to the learning styles inventory on pages 67-68. Ask those who completed the inventory to share what they discovered about their learning styles.

7. Invite those who brought books to share titles and brief synopses. Identify books available "on loan." Set a date when owners may expect their return.

8. Mention study opportunities available through your church. Distribute written information, if available.

9. Encourage mentoring as another valuable approach to gaining wisdom and insight. Note the difference between a nudger (an informal, often peer-based, and long-term relationship) and a mentor (a more formal, usually older to younger, time-dated relationship). Resources for mentoring are available from your LifeWay Christian Store or Baptist Book Store.

Closing the Session

1. Repeat together *This Week's Verse* on page 57. Ask moms to share sentence testimonies of God's truths that have guided them in decision making. Affirm Jesus as the Way, the Truth, and the Life (see John 14:6).

2. Lead a prayer thanking God that He is a faithful and trustworthy Guide.

Session 6

Help: Sometimes I Need to Share the Load

Before the Session

1. On three signs, write one each of the following descriptive phrases: (1) The Doer; (2) The Coordinator; (3) The Procrastinator.

2. Arrange chairs in three circles around the room. On the floor in the middle of each circle, place one of the descriptive signs.

2. Ask your pastor to identify local counselors who are sources of emotional help for moms. Compile a list and copy one for each mom.

During the Session

1. As moms sign in, ask them to sit in the circle that best represents their personalities. When everyone is seated, introduce the activity by saying: *Each circle represents a personality style. Circle 1 is the Type A, driven, task-oriented style. Some key phrases are "I'd rather burn out than rust out," and "Any job worth doing is worth doing right."*

    Circle 2 is the person who loves to administer, organize, and coordinate the work of others. She is person-centered, not task-centered. Her key phrase is "United we stand, divided we fall." This person will do most any task if someone else is working alongside. She dislikes working alone.

    Circle 3 is the playful, spontaneous person who can always find a good reason to postpone unpleasant tasks. Although her home may be cluttered and she can't find her daytimer, her key phrase is "Tomorrow, tomorrow, there's always tomorrow." Chaos seems normal—even fun!

    In light of the explanation, allow moms to change circles. Then, ask members of each circle to explain how their styles impact the need discussed in Week 6.

    Then, lead moms to identify and discuss what they can learn from personality styles other than their own to help them more effectively manage their time and stress levels. (This conversation may take the entire group time. If not, continue with the following activities.)

2. Assign each circle one of the following sources of help: parenting partners; husbands; children. Direct them to review Week 6 for suggestions related to each of these sources. Allow circles to report to the group options that have worked well for them.

3. As a group, discuss the implications of not asking for help. Read aloud Hebrews 12:9-10. Summarize by saying: *The discipline of helping is an important part of effective parenting. Our role is to work ourselves out of a job by teaching children independence and self-reliance.*

4. *Optional:* Distribute the list of counselors. Commend counseling as an appropriate source of emotional support for moms.

Closing the Session

1. Review "The Ultimate Helper" from page 80. Repeat together *This Week's Verse* and the *Mothering Maxim* on page 69.

2. Lead a prayer for God's guidance as moms seek to implement the truths of this study.

Session 7
Recreation: Sometimes I Need a Break

Before the Session

1. Decorate the room with toys, sports equipment, crafts, or other recreational reminders.

2. Enlist someone to demonstrate or tell about child-safety equipment that allows children to participate with their parents in recreational activities (biking, hiking, roller blading, jogging, etc.).

During the Session

1. As moms sign in, ask them to select an item from the room that illustrates a favorite form of play. Suggest they hold the items in their laps until called on in group time.

2. Ask moms to explain why they chose the item they did, or what item they would have chosen had it been available. Summarize the

importance of play in a well-balanced life. Be sensitive to anyone who may struggle to accept the need for play. Call for testimonies of how recreation plays a vital role in stress reduction and holistic health.

3. *Optional:* Say, *Children, with the right safety precautions, can accompany us as we play.* Introduce the person prepared to discuss or demonstrate child-safety equipment.

4. Point out that recreation does not have to be expensive. Call for moms' reactions to the activity at the top of page 87.

5. Give moms the opportunity to share ways they schedule physical fitness during their daily or weekly routines. Mention other beneficial health habits, such as those listed at the bottom of page 88. Ask if anyone has opted

to begin the Six-Week Starter program provided on page 89.

6. Invite volunteers to share examples of family fun activities, including family rituals (p. 92). Share a personal response to the activity at the bottom of page 92 before inviting others to respond.

Closing the Session

1. Review the need to feed our spirits. Encourage moms to consider the prayer walk activity on page 90. If possible, plan a group prayer walk.

2. Repeat together the *Mothering Maxim* and *This Week's Verse* from page 81.

3. Call on a volunteer to lead a prayer thanking God for refreshing our spirits through this study.

Session 8
Perspective: Sometimes I Lose My Focus

Before the Session

1. Prepare three signs containing one of the following words: past, present, future. Display one sign on each of three walls.

2. If possible, call moms and remind them to bring a stress sack to the session.

During the Session

1. Ask, *What do we mean by perspective?* After several responses, ask, *Why is keeping perspective so difficult?* Read or say together the *Mothering Maxim* on page 93.

2. Ask moms to stand by one of the three signs that most represents where they focus the majority of their thoughts. Lead them to examine the implications of each pattern and to determine a healthy balance.

3. Invite volunteers to share the "mothering myths" that have affected how they mother (p. 100). Emphasize that these are myths and need to be discarded. Then ask volunteers to share realities that are valuable to remember and practice.

4. Call attention to the circus analogy on page 101. Emphasize the truth of the margin Scripture, Jeremiah 29:11. Select a volunteer to read aloud Matthew 11:28-29. Say, *When our burden does not feel light, perhaps it is because we are carrying more than God intended.*

5. Ask those who brought a stress sack to share the items and their meanings with the group. Express appreciation to participants.

6. Invite responses to the closing activity on page 104. Read together the essay, "A New Day."

Closing the Session

1. Lead a directed prayer, allowing moms to pray silently as you mention the following topics: what I am grateful for in the past; what I relish in the present; what I anticipate in the future. Close the prayer time by thanking God for His marvelous plan for our lives. Ask Him to give us His perspective on mothering, as well as all that we do.

2. Remind moms of the truth of *This Week's Verse* on page 93. Review the activity on page 101. Say the verse together.

Session 9
Hope: Sometimes I Wonder if There Is More to Life

Before the Session

1. Enlist one or more moms to share their salvation testimonies and to describe how having Jesus as their Lord impacts daily life.

2. If you are aware of an unsaved mom in your group, attempt to spend some time with her when she has completed Week 9 to discuss her reaction/readiness to make a profession of faith. Do not solicit this information during the session. If it is not possible to get together prior to the session, do so as a follow-up to the study.

During the Session

1. Repeat together the *Mothering Maxim* on page 105. Affirm the truth of this definition of hope.

2. Refer to pages 106-107 and discuss the four sources we often turn to for hope. As a group, determine why these sources represent misplaced hope.

3. Call on the person(s) enlisted to share a testimony. Thank each one who shares.

4. Ask someone who keeps a prayer journal to explain how this activity enhances her faith.

5. Call attention to pages 110-111 and discuss the stumbling blocks to faith. Review the descriptions of faith. Point out the necessity of prayer, listening to God, and Bible study as essential elements of building faith and hope.

6. As time permits, review the nine needs and growth plans moms listed on page 115.

Closing the Session

1. Commend those who have served as prayer partners during the study. Suggest they continue to pray for one another as memories of the group surface during the coming weeks.

2. Ask the group to stand and form a circle. One-by-one, direct each mom to stand in the circle as another mom prays for her.

3. Thank each person for her contribution to the group. Remind moms of other study opportunities in coming weeks. As a closing benediction, repeat *This Week's Verse* on page 105.